Thomas Hauser on Sports

BOOKS BY THOMAS HAUSER

GENERAL NON-FICTION

Missing

The Trial of Patrolman Thomas Shea

For Our Children (with Frank Macchiarola)

The Family Legal Companion

Final Warning: The Legacy of Chernobyl (with Dr. Robert Gale)

Arnold Palmer: A Personal Journey

Confronting America's Moral Crisis (with Frank Macchiarola)

Healing: A Journal of Tolerance and Understanding

Miscellaneous

With This Ring (with Frank Macchiarola)

A God To Hope For

Thomas Hauser on Sports

BOXING NON-FICTION

The Black Lights: Inside the World of Professional Boxing

Muhammad Ali: His Life and Times

Muhammad Ali: Memories

Muhammad Ali: In Perspective

Muhammad Ali & Company

A Beautiful Sickness

A Year At The Fights

Brutal Artistry

The View From Ringside

Chaos, Corruption, Courage, and Glory

The Lost Legacy of Muhammad Ali

I Don't Believe It, But It's True

Knockout (with Vikki LaMotta)

The Greatest Sport of All

The Boxing Scene

An Unforgiving Sport

Boxing Is . . .

Box: The Face of Boxing

The Legend of Muhammad Ali (with Bart Barry)

Winks and Daggers

And the New . . .

FICTION

Ashworth & Palmer

Agatha's Friends

The Beethoven Conspiracy

Hanneman's War

The Fantasy

Dear Hannah

The Hawthorne Group

Mark Twain Remembers

Finding The Princess

Waiting For Carver Boyd

FOR CHILDREN

Martin Bear & Friends

Thomas Hauser on Sports

Remembering the Journey

Thomas Hauser

The University of Arkansas Press
Fayetteville
2013

ISBN-10: 1-55728-635-3
ISBN-13: 978-1-55728-635-2
e-ISBN: 978-1-61075-524-5

17   16   15   14   13   5   4   3   2   1

⊗The paper used in this publication meets the minimum requirements of the
American National Standard for Permanence of Paper for Printed Library Materials
Z39.48-1984.

Library of Congress Cataloging-in-Publication Data

Hauser, Thomas.
   Thomas Hauser on sports : remembering the journey / Thomas Hauser.
      pages cm
   ISBN 978-1-55728-635-2 (pbk. : alk. paper)
   1. Sport—United States—History. I. Title.
   GV583.H38 2013
   796.0973—dc23
                                                                    2013004846

For Seth Abraham

Contents

A Word of Introduction   ix

When the World Was Young   1
A Yankee Fan Grows Older   6
"Hello, Kid": A Conversation with Babe Ruth   9
When Time Stopped for Baseball   13
The Greatest Baseball Game Ever Played   16
Hero   20
Jerry Izenberg: An Appreciation   25
Bill Bradley Remembered   31
Wilt Chamberlain (1936–1999)   34
Ted Williams (1918–2002)   38
Howard Cosell (1918–1995)   42
Arthur Ashe (1943–1993)   45
Are Baseball Players Happy?: A Personal Memory of Marvin Miller   49
Arnold Palmer at Seventy-Five   60
The Political Side of Arnold Palmer   67
Invite Everyone to the Dance   70
The Ten Greatest Moments in American Sports   73
The Westminster Kennel Club Dog Show   78
Extreme-Ultimate-No-Holds-Barred Fighting   84
Sport Magazine and Those Total Encyclopedias   89
Upset ! ! !   92
Larry Merchant: Play 42   107
Black and White and *Sports Illustrated*'s "Sportsman of the Year"   112
Hypocrisy at West Point   116
West Point Revisited   119
Tim McCarver   127
If Disaster Strikes   136
The NFL Overtime Rule   142
Roar, Lion, Roar: Columbia Football   145
Columbia Basketball   149

Columbia Baseball   153

I've Been to the Mountaintop: A Sports Fan Is Painted by
　　LeRoy Neiman   157

Mickey Mantle: A Personal Remembrance   163

Marv Albert: "Yesss!"   166

Pete Rose: A Meeting Remembered   169

Baseball's Steroid Problem   176

In the Press Box   182

Courtside with David Diamante   186

I Could Always Hit a Baseball   190

Destroying the High Temple   194

Long Ago at Madison Square Garden   198

A Word of Introduction

My first love was baseball. Over the years, I've achieved recognition as a boxing writer. But long before I turned to the sweet science, "America's national pastime" captured my heart. I followed boxing, but only as a casual fan. Other sports meant more to me.

My childhood allegiance was to the New York Yankees. Growing up in the suburbs of New York, I also cheered for the Giants (in football), Rangers (hockey), and Knicks (basketball). In college, the often-hapless Columbia Lions became my cause.

In recent years, boxing has moved center stage in my professional life. But I look back fondly on the days of my youth when other sports meant so much to me. This book recounts my journey through those sports and some of the people I've met in them.

Thomas Hauser
New York, N.Y.
2013

As I noted in this article for Sports Illustrated, there was a time when nostalgia was a feeling that reflected the innocent side of sports; not a business.

When the World Was Young

In January 1962, Milwaukee Braves pitcher Warren Spahn changed my life. I was fifteen years old, an avid sports fan who read everything I could about baseball. A magazine had just published an article about Spahn with one of the nicest photographs I'd ever seen. It showed the Milwaukee Braves pitcher from the chest up, in uniform against a bright red backdrop, smiling directly at the camera.

That same week, there was another photograph of Spahn in the *New York Herald Tribune*. He was on a makeshift pitcher's mound, wearing sweatclothes and spikes, with his right leg kicking high in the air. The caption said that Spahn was getting in shape for the upcoming season by working out at his home in Hartshorne, Oklahoma.

Something in my mind clicked. I'd sporadically collected autographs before. Now, hoping against hope, I put the magazine photo in a nine-by-twelve-inch manila envelope with a piece of shirt cardboard to keep the photo from bending. I added a self-addressed stamped return envelope and a note telling Spahn that I was a fan and would be eternally grateful if he autographed the photo and sent it back to me. Then, trusting in the omniscience of the United States postal delivery system, I mailed it to "Warren Spahn, Hartshorne, Oklahoma."

Ten days later, my return envelope came back. Spahn's picture was inside. He was smiling at me. And across his chest, in blue ink, were the words: "TO TOM HAUSER, BEST WISHES, WARREN SPAHN."

I freaked. I'd never gotten anything that good in the mail before. Warren Spahn had written to me. And then that something in my mind clicked again. I had a baseball yearbook that featured every major league roster and listed every player's hometown. Some of the players lived in large cities, but others came from rural areas. Richie Ashburn lived in

Tilden, Nebraska. Roger Maris, who had hit sixty-one home runs the previous year, made his home in Raytown, Missouri. Going through my collection of magazines, I tore out the photos of ten players who came from small towns and mailed them out. Then, when the baseball season began, I repeated the process, sending photos to players in care of their respective teams. Each mailing cost eight cents in postage, plus another six cents for the return fare. My father provided the manila envelopes. The shirt cardboards came from the laundry. My early mailings were usually to baseball players because those were the color photos that sports magazines most often carried. But I wrote to anyone whose full-page photo I had. And every day after school, I came home to check for nine-by-twelve-inch return envelopes in the mail.

The world was different in 1962. Professional sports was still in its infancy as far as salaries, television, and other marketing factors were concerned. Westward expansion had just begun. Large network television contracts were unknown. Marvin Miller was with the steelworkers' union. Kids wore sneakers, not hundred-dollar specialty shoes. College sports were presumed to be pure.

But more important, from a boy's point of view, sports memorabilia was collected for fun. Baseball cards were traded and flipped, not stored in plastic binders. The idea of an auction at Sotheby's was so foreign to sports as to be absurd.

The ballplayers were different, too. Ninety percent of the photos I sent out were returned; in most instances, with obvious care. Many of my heroes put their own return address in the upper left-hand corner of the reply envelope. Others wrote, "Photo / Do not bend," on the outside. Quite a few—Roberto Clemente, Len Dawson, Bobby Hull, Bill Mazeroski, Maurice Richard, and Jim Taylor, to name a few—enclosed photos of their own in addition to the one I'd sent. Others enclosed reply letters. Mel Allen wrote that he was "quite flattered that you have asked for my autograph." Larry Wilson thanked me for the kindness of enclosing a return envelope. Most of the players didn't just sign their names. They took care to write something special on their photo—"To Tom . . . Best Wishes . . . Good Luck . . ."

Dizzy Dean and Jack Dempsey both wrote that I was their "pal." So did Sugar Ray Robinson. Gene Mauch signed a photo that showed him arguing with an umpire with the words, "I'm telling you, Tom Hauser is my friend." Sonny Liston wrote, "Best regard [*sic*] from Sonny Liston." Being somewhat sullen at times, Sonny obviously gave his regards out sparingly. Later, I got a second photo from Liston on which "best" was crossed out and rewritten because initially it had been misspelled.

Many of the athletes I wrote to were generous with their time. Raymond Berry, then an All-Pro receiver with the Baltimore Colts, signed, "To Tom, with best personal regards, Raymond Berry, John 3:1-18." This was before it was fashionable for ballplayers to wear their religion on their sleeve, so I wrote Berry back, asking why he had signed with a reference to the Bible. Over the next year, he sent me three long letters explaining his philosophy of life.

Another time, I mailed out what I thought were two photos of Baltimore Orioles pitcher Steve Barber. Barber returned both of them. He'd autographed one, and as his cover letter explained, "The other one isn't me; it's Milt Pappas." And sure enough, Barber had gotten Pappas (his teammate) to autograph the other.

But no response was more generous than the one I received from Vince Lombardi. *Life* magazine had run a story about the Green Bay Packers with a fold-out cover showing the famed Green Bay sweep. I mailed it to Lombardi for his autograph, since I thought he best epitomized football's greatest team. Hard-hearted Vince Lombardi returned the cover autographed by every member of the Packers.

One by one, the pictures I collected went into frames on my bedroom walls. Eventually, I ran out of space, and I began to store them in envelopes in my closet. Over the years, I collected more than five hundred photos from over three hundred different sports heroes. Then I got "too old for that sort of thing," and my collecting days came to an end.

Recently, there was an auction of sports memorabilia at Sotheby's. A Honus Wagner baseball card sold for $451,000. Over two days, the auction grossed more than $5,000,000. Reading about the sale, I thought of my photos. I still have them, in a closet, although I've moved several times. So I took out the envelopes and began to look at pictures I hadn't seen for decades.

There was Hank Aaron, Ted Williams, Stan Musial, and Jackie Robinson. Also, Max Alvis, Sam Mele, Woodie Held, and Pete Ward. In retrospect, most of the players look very young. When they'd autographed the pictures, they were younger than I am now.

Then I began making lists. I had autographed photos from thirty-three members of baseball's Hall of Fame. There were twenty-nine MVP's, ten different Cy Young Award winners, twenty-one home run champions, and nineteen players who had won batting titles. Eight of my signatories had three thousand or more base hits. Ten had hit more than five hundred home runs. Six of my pitchers had won three hundred games. And that was just baseball. Fifteen of my photos were from players now in the Basketball Hall of Fame. Thirty-five of my football correspondents were enshrined in Canton. Not to mention the superstars from other sports—Bobby Jones, Ben Hogan, Sam Snead, Jack Nicklaus, Arnold Palmer, Rafer Johnson, Willie Shoemaker, Gordie Howe, and Cassius Marcellus Clay Jr. before he changed his name.

It was inevitable, of course, that I would ask that horrible question: "How much are my pictures worth?"

Harlan J. Werner is the chairman of AW Sports in Irvine, California. "It's a nice collection," Werner told me after I'd compiled a master list and faxed it to him. "But there are several factors to keep in mind."

"Like what?" I queried.

"Well, first, in this business you have to consider the nature of the item signed. For example, Joe DiMaggio's signature on a baseball bat is worth several thousand dollars. That's because he refuses to sign them. DiMaggio on a baseball is worth two hundred dollars. On an eight-by-ten-inch *real* photo, seventy-five dollars. Your DiMaggio autograph is only on a picture from a magazine, which makes it worth about forty dollars. That's what Joe charges for his signature at a card show."

"Also," Werner continued, "I should warn you, some of your signatures are probably phony. Back in the sixties, Mickey Mantle had the clubhouse boy or a club secretary sign for him. After Roy Campanella had his car accident, his wife did almost all his signing. Now if you want verification . . ."

Feeling like a six-year-old who has just been told that Santa Claus doesn't exist, I made my next call to Mike Gutierrez (co-owner of MVP Autographs and Sports Memorabilia). Werner had assured me that Gutierrez knows as much about sports autographs as anyone in the business."

To my relief, Gutierrez expressed the view that most of my signatures are "probably real." Like Werner, he thinks that about a third of my pictures have "value." A lot of them are of superstars, and it's economically fortuitous that some of the signers have died. My most valuable picture, if the autograph is genuine, is of Bill Russell, who simply refuses to sign autographs. I know my Russell signature is real, because he gave it to me in person outside the Celtics' locker room at Madison Square Garden before I ever wrote to Warren Spahn. It's now worth five hundred dollars. My photo of Bobby Jones is also in the five-hundred-dollar range, as is my Green Bay Packers *Life* magazine cover. Roberto Clemente, Cassius Clay, Lew Alcindor, Sonny Liston, Jackie Robinson, Roger Maris, and Walter O'Malley are each worth several hundred dollars. By contrast, my Hank Aarons are worth only ten to fifteen dollars each, which is a shame because I have eight of them, dating back to when Aaron had 253 home runs.

All totaled, Gutierrez thinks my collection is worth well into five figures. But the truth is, for me, its value can't be measured in dollars. Looking at the photos as I did last week, just for a moment I was young again. Once more, I was fifteen years old, in communion with Warren Spahn. Spahn was smiling at me. And I gave thanks for his kindness, which led to the fulfillment of a boy's dream.

Revisiting the touchstones of one's youth can bring mixed emotions

A Yankee Fan Grows Older

Once upon a time, believe it or not, doubleheaders were regularly scheduled by the lords of baseball. In 1961 (the year Roger Maris hit sixty-one home runs), the New York Yankees played twelve Sunday double-headers at home. A box seat cost $3.50. General admission was $1.30. The bleachers were under a dollar. I was fifteen years old at the time. I know I'm starting to sound like an old fogey. But for older Americans, baseball, more than any other sport, is deeply ingrained in memories of childhood, so bear with me for a moment while I reminisce.

When I was a boy, I'd go to ten doubleheaders a year; all of them at Yankee Stadium. My friends and I would arrive ninety minutes early to get good seats in the upper deck and watch batting practice. There were four Hall of Famers in the Yankee lineup—Mickey Mantle, Yogi Berra, Whitey Ford, and Phil Rizzuto. And I saw countless others headed for Cooperstown—Ted Williams, Al Kaline, Harmon Killebrew, Luis Aparicio, Nellie Fox, Early Wynn.

One of my happiest moments came when I went to a Yankees-Tigers doubleheader and the first game lasted fifteen innings. In those long-ago days, there was no place on Earth I'd rather be. I knew I was starting to get old when I went to a doubleheader at the stadium with some friends during my second year of law school. Around the middle of the second game, I started to wish it would end. Now I go to a game once every few years.

That brings me to July 4, 2000. Once upon a time, the Fourth of July was a day of particular significance in baseball. Whoever was in first place on July 4, it was said, would most likely win the pennant. This year, the Yankees were playing the Baltimore Orioles at the stadium. It seemed like a good day for me to revisit my childhood, so I took the subway up to the Bronx.

As one grows older, perceptions change, but Yankee Stadium is still awe inspiring. As for the game itself, it's no secret that the Bronx Bombers have been struggling this season. Starting pitching has been the reason why, and July 4 was no different. David Cone was on the mound, and he surrendered home runs to Mike Bordick, Harold Baines, Brady Anderson, and Mark Lewis. That accounted for seven Oriole runs, which was all Baltimore needed. A ninth-inning Yankee rally fell short, and the Bombers lost 7–6. The dramatic highpoint of the afternoon came during the fifth inning, when a voice on the stadium public-address system intoned "it's proposal time" and announced that an ardent suitor wanted to know, "Alicia, will you marry me?" At that moment, it seemed as though virtually all of the 44,447 fans in attendance shouted "NO!" It would be nice to think that Alicia said, "Yes."

The weather was hot and humid. Around the middle of the sixth inning, I started to wish the game would end. Still, it was obvious that, for the multitude of children sitting nearby, the entire experience was magical.

I don't know when I'll go to Yankee Stadium again. Baseball is now vibrant and exciting for me only in memory. But those memories will always be with me. And in tribute to them, I'd like to bequeath to younger generations a list of things that I recall most fondly about baseball the way it used to be:

(1) Irregularly-shaped playing fields with foul lines that were "too short" and centerfields so large that you could put monuments there and not interfere with play.

(2) Crowds that cheered without the aid of "tomahawk chops," "homer hankies," or electronic scoreboards that trumpet "Charge!"

(3) The policy of holding back general-admission seats until the day of a game, so anyone (and particularly children) who cared enough could go to the ballpark early and get tickets for a crucial game.

(4) Starting pitchers who finished what they started and were allowed to bat for themselves.

(5) Managers who didn't play the percentages with switch-hitters ad nauseam.

(6) Baseball cards that were flipped, traded, and carried in back pockets instead of being put in binders by eight-year-olds as an investment.

(7) Jackie Robinson, Stan Musial, Sandy Koufax, Warren Spahn, Ernie Banks, Willie Mays, and (especially) Ted Williams.

(8) World Series day games (and the Gillette theme song: "To look sharp . . .").

(9) 714 . . . 2,130 . . . 4,191

(10) Being young enough that every game mattered enormously to me; even the All–Star Game.

For many baseball fans, Babe Ruth is still the overriding mythic personality in sports.

"Hello, Kid":
A Conversation with Babe Ruth

Babe Ruth: Hello, kid. What can I do for you?

Q: Well, sir; I'm writing an article, and I wondered if I could ask you a few questions.

Babe Ruth: Fire away.

Q: Thank you, sir. The first question I have is, do you play baseball up in heaven?

Babe Ruth: Do we play baseball? Kid, this is heaven. Of course we play baseball.

Q: Is it organized, like a league?

Babe Ruth: It is a league. In fact, there's two leagues with eight teams each. That's sixteen teams altogether. We only play day games and there are doubleheaders on Sunday. The ballparks are the way they used to be; no Astroturf or any of that stuff. And in Celestial baseball, the pennant races mean something. There's no divisional playoff or league championship series. If your team finishes in first place, you go to the World Series.

Q: Are the teams like the ones on Earth?

Babe Ruth: Like the ones on Earth used to be. We've got the New York Yankees, the Brooklyn Dodgers, Washington Senators, all the way down the line, with a special draft for players from the old Negro League.

Q: Which team do you play for?

Babe Ruth: The Yankees, of course.

Q: Who are the best players in Celestial baseball?

Babe Ruth: Well, kid. Not to be immodest or anything; but there's me and then there's everyone else.

Q: What about Ty Cobb?

Babe Ruth: Cobb didn't make it. He's playing in an outlaw league down south.

Q: Who are the toughest pitchers for you to hit?

Babe Ruth: Walter Johnson and Satchel Paige. But to be honest with you, up here, everyone is tough. To play in this league, you've got to be good. Last year, we played the New York Giants in the World Series. How'd you like to go up against a rotation that includes Christy Mathewson, Joe McGinnity, Rube Marquard, and Carl Hubbell. We had a rookie come up to the league this season; a kid named Drysdale. In spring training, I figured I'd intimidate him. You know; do my 1932 World Series call-my-shot-by-waving-to-the-bleachers thing. Sonofabitch stuck a fastball in my ear.

Q: Are you leading the league in home runs?

A: Hell, yes. 1949 was my first full season up here, and I've averaged 51 homers a year since then. So far, I've hit 2,625 home runs against Celestial-quality pitching. Let Henry Aaron top that.

Q: How good are the Yankees?

A: Our manager is Joe McCarthy. We got Lou Gehrig at first; Tony Lazzeri at second; Bill Dickey behind the plate; Red Ruffing and Lefty Gomez on the mound. The outfield is Mickey Mantle in left, Joe DiMaggio in center, and yours truly in right. Does that answer your question?

Q: In other words, it's "Damn Yankees" all over again.

Babe Ruth: Right you are, kid. By the way, DiMaggio is a good ballplayer, but he's a pain in the ass. He got here last year. And right away, the first game he played in, he wanted to be introduced as "the greatest living ballplayer." We explained to him, "Joe, up here, you're just a rookie. And besides, if you want to get technical about it, you're dead." Finally, we got that settled, and then Joe found out that Marilyn Monroe was living with Rogers Hornsby. Boy, was he pissed.

Q: What about the other teams?

Babe Ruth: They're all good. Used to be that folks would laugh when they went into Pittsburgh. Now you go to Forbes Field, and they've got Honus Wagner, Pie Traynor, Paul Waner, Roberto Clemente, and a bunch of guys like Josh Gibson, Jimmie Crutchfield, and Double-Duty Radcliffe who played for the Pittsburgh Crawfords in the old Negro League.

Q: Do you follow Major League Baseball today?

Babe Ruth: Oh, yeah. We get all the stations. Bob Costas and Tim McCarver are my favorite living announcers. But to be honest with you, I'm partial to the old-timers. Mel Allen and Red Barber do play-by-play for the Yankees here in heaven. There's nothing I enjoy more than Mel Allen shouting, "Ruth swings, and there's a drive to deep right field . . . It's going . . . Going . . . Gone! . . . A Ballantine blast!"

Q: What do you think of Howard Cosell?

Babe Ruth: I don't get to hear him much. He broadcasts games for the league that Cobb plays in.

Q: What do you think of the players on Earth today?

Babe Ruth: They're good. McGwire and Sosa are fun to watch; although I've got suspicions about certain things. And I should remind you, in 1927, the year I hit sixty home runs, I hit more home runs than any other TEAM in the American League. And I like watching some of the other youngsters. Cal Ripken Jr. is a gamer.

Q: A real throwback; right?

Babe Ruth: Sure, kid. By the way, I forgot to mention, Lou Gehrig played his first game in the Celestial League in 1941. Since then, he's played in 9,086 consecutive regular-season contests.

Children growing up today will have their own World Series memories.
But they'll be very different from mine.

When Time Stopped for Baseball

During childhood, when baseball most mattered to me, I was a Yankees fan.

It was a glorious era. I was born in 1946; and during a sixteen-year period from 1949 through 1964, the Yankees were in the World Series fourteen times.

The Yankees I grew up with were epitomized by Mickey Mantle, Yogi Berra, and Whitey Ford. But I was a big clumsy kid. So at age six, when I got my first baseball uniform, I wore number 36 in honor Johnny Mize, who shared first-base duties with Joe Collins. Then Mize retired and, in 1954, I switched to 53, the number worn by Bill "Moose" Skowron during his rookie year.

Decades later, I was at a cocktail party when a man in his mid-sixties, who was looking for someone to talk with, came over and introduced himself. He was stocky with a fighter's face and military haircut that seemed out of place in the 1990s. "Hi, buddy," he said, extending his hand. "Moose Skowron."

And my heart skipped a beat.

I told him he'd been one of my childhood heroes and that I'd worn number 53 when all the other kids were wearing 7. That pleased him. It wasn't often that he met someone who'd favored him over Mickey Mantle. We talked for a while. Skowron was no longer the god I'd remembered. His doctor had just ordered him to stop eating red meat. "I don't know if life is worth living without steak," Moose told me.

And in that moment, my mind flashed back to the seventh game of the 1956 World Series. New York Yankees versus the Brooklyn Dodgers. Bases loaded . . . Moose Skowron at bat . . . "There's a drive to deep left field; way way back . . ."

It was a grand slam home run. The Yankees won. I remembered it well. I heard it.

To repeat: I heard it. Because in 1956, the World Series was accessible to children.

Some of my most vivid baseball memories are of listening to the World Series in grade-school classrooms. Our teachers had the ultimate weapon at their command. With one act, they could ensure discipline and concentration. They could even make us adore them. The carrot was, "If you're good and work hard this morning, you can listen to the World Series in the afternoon." The stick was, "If you're less than perfect, you can't."

We'd worked diligently until the first pitch, which (if memory serves me correctly) was unleashed at 1:00 PM. At that point, the radio went on. We listened to the game until school let out. Then we ran home and watched the last few innings on television. THE catch by Willie Mays in deep centerfield; Don Larsen's perfect game; Bill Mazeroski's series-clinching home run; the line drive off the bat of Willie McCovey that Bobby Richardson caught. I soared to incredible heights with some of those moments and died little deaths with others.

Eventually, my interest in baseball waned. It's no longer the most important thing in the world to me. But part of the hold that the sport continues to have over me is that it's a game of tradition. Over the decades, there has been only measured change.

Put today's National Basketball Association teams against their predecessors from a half-century ago and you'd have a massacre. Ditto for a contest between current National Football League squads and early NFL teams. But reaching back to the early decades of the last century, Walter Johnson and Christy Mathewson could compete on a baseball field today. Ty Cobb could still play the game.

The biggest changes have come in the ambiance of the sport. Baseball isn't played in "ballparks" anymore. Games are contested in stadiums with super-amplified rock music. There's too much noise competing with the crack of bat against ball and the roar of the crowd. And more significantly, during the World Series, night baseball reigns supreme.

The first major league baseball game to be played at night was in Cincinnati on May 24, 1935. Franklin Roosevelt pushed a button in the White House to turn on the lights at Crosley Field. Initially, each team was limited to seven home night games a year. Then, in 1942, in deference to American factory workers involved in the World War II military effort, that number was raised to fourteen.

Meanwhile, a little-known medium called television was in its infancy. The first major league baseball game to be televised was the opener of a doubleheader between the Brooklyn Dodgers and Cincinnati Reds at Ebbets Field on August 26, 1939. The game was telecast over station W2XBS to the handful of TV sets that existed in the New York metropolitan area. Red Barber was the announcer. As late as 1950, 65 million Americans listened to the World Series on radio, while only 20 million watched it on television.

Times change. In game four of the 1971 World Series between the Pittsburgh Pirates and Baltimore Orioles, the lights went on for the first time in postseason play. Every World Series game since 1985 has been played at night.

That's sad. Baseball is a summer game. In late-October, unless the home team plays inside a dome or in a warm-weather climate, conditions are likely to be cold, wet, windy, and raw. Players sit in the dugout, wearing ski caps, gloves, and thermal jackets. Each breath that escapes their lips turns the air frosty white. The quality of play is adversely affected. And scheduling baseball's showcase event entirely at night has a significant impact on children.

As I write these words, the Boston Red Sox are no longer cursed. They won the World Series an hour ago, defeating the St. Louis Cardinals for their first world championship since 1918 (the year Ted Williams was born).

Unfortunately, most children missed it, just as they missed seeing Boston's thrilling comeback from a three-games-to-none deficit against the New York Yankees in the American League Championship Series last week. That's because World Series games now begin when many children on the East Coast are getting ready for bed and often extend past midnight.

I understand the economic imperatives of playing at night. But I can't help but think that eliminating World Series day games completely has taken away another piece of the magical world of being a child. It's one of the reasons that more and more children today grow up playing games other than baseball. And it's not just future stars of the game who are being lost. Future fans are being lost too.

Television doesn't know any better, but Major League Baseball should. At the very least, the lords of the realm should give fans a weekend World Series day game.

My love of sports began as a child, and escalated when my uncle took me to my first major league baseball game.

The Greatest Baseball Game
Ever Played

A panel of sportswriters met recently to select "The Greatest Baseball Game Ever Played." The results were predictable. Bobby Thomson's miracle home run; Don Larson's perfect game; Boston 7, Cincinnati 6 in the sixth game of the 1975 World Series. It's too bad no one asked for my vote because, if they had, I could have told them that The Greatest Baseball Game Ever Played took place on July 31, 1953. I know, because I was there. The New York Yankees clobbered the St. Louis Browns 11 to 5. I was seven years old, and it was the first major league baseball game I ever attended.

Baseball in 1953 was on the verge of radical change. Prior to the season, schedule approval for the entire American League was delayed when St. Louis Browns president Bill Veeck demanded that the New York Yankees share their revenue from televised night games with other teams. Then a group of players banded together and hired a New York City attorney named J. N. Lewis to serve as their legal representative in dealings with club owners. Lewis was promptly barred by Commissioner Ford Frick from attending executive council meetings. Later that year, the United States Supreme Court ruled that baseball was a sport, not a business, and thus not subject to the nation's antitrust laws.

Other laws were also considered inapplicable to the great American game. On April 6, the Hot Springs, Arkansas, baseball team was dropped from the Cotton States League because it signed a black pitcher named Jim Tugerson to a team contract. Several court hearings later, league president Al Haraway rescinded the ouster but, still flaunting the United States Constitution, ordered the forfeiture of all games in which Tugerson played. Meanwhile, in another part of the Deep South, a nineteen-year-old named Henry Aaron was on his way to becoming MVP in the Sally League.

More important than all of the above, however, was the fact that the magical world of major league baseball was about to unfold before my eyes. My uncle was taking me to my first game.

Like many New Yorkers, I was avidly pro-Yankee. After all, it isn't often that a seven-year-old can root for a team in quest of its fifth World Championship in five years. The Bomber pitching staff started with Whitey Ford and included Ed Lopat, Allie Reynolds, and Johnny Sain. Mickey Mantle was in the lineup, surrounded by Yogi Berra, Phil Rizzuto, and Johnny Mize.

By contrast, the Browns (who would leave St. Louis for Baltimore the following year) were a sorry lot en route to a last-place record of 54 wins and 100 losses. Their leading hitter was Dick Kryhoski with a .278 average. Their top pitcher, Marlin Stuart, would win all of eight games that year.

Still, the 1953 Yanks and Browns were capable of playing exciting baseball against one another. Their first encounter, which ended in a ten-inning 7–6 New York triumph, featured a seventeen-minute bench-clearing brawl that began when St. Louis catcher Clint Courtney spiked Yankee shortstop Phil Rizzuto with a high slide at second base. Plate umpire Bill Summers called the battle "a real beauty, the best I've ever seen." American League president Will Harridge took a dimmer view, fining Courtney $250. Billy Martin of the Yankees was fined $150 for, in Harridge's words, "continuing the brawl when it appeared to be over."

That was the first Yankees-Browns match-up. In the second, the Yanks won 6–5 in ten innings, but not before the two clubs set a major league mark by using a combined total of forty-one players. Then, on June 16 at Yankee Stadium, the lowly Browns rose up and smote the Yankees 3 to 1. The victory snapped a fourteen-game Browns losing streak and, more important, ended the Bombers' victory string at eighteen games (one shy of the American League record). Clearly, St. Louis was a rival to be reckoned with.

As for the game itself, some memories have been lost to time, but others remain. Jim MacDonald pitched for New York; Marlin Stuart for the Browns. I was very confused by my initial sighting of Yankee Stadium, which looked from the outside like a big building without grass, totally unlike the school playground where I was used to seeing baseball played. I recall surprise at the absence of play-by-play commentary by Mel Allen.

And I remember one moment of serious apprehension when my uncle left me alone in my seat while he went to the men's room.

Everything else was superb. The Yankees scored three times in the first inning and loaded the bases with none out in the second. Then Mickey Mantle strode to the plate. Three months earlier, the heir apparent to Joe DiMaggio had unloaded a mammoth home run off Washington's Chuck Stobbs to pace a 7–3 Yankee victory. The ball, which came to rest in the backyard of a house 565 feet from home plate, was second in distance only to a prodigious 600-foot wallop by Babe Ruth in Detroit's Briggs Stadium twenty-seven years earlier. Now (I assured my uncle) Mantle was about to unload a grand-slam wallop, which might even be the first fair ball ever hit out of Yankee Stadium.

I remember the Mantle-Stuart confrontation well because it was the dramatic high point of my baseball-viewing career. Everything was in place. Bases loaded, Mantle at the plate, Marlin Stuart cowering with fear. Right at that moment, Stuart reached into his pocket, took out a handkerchief, and wiped his brow. It was a classic gesture of surrender by a man who looked very much like he didn't want to pitch to Mickey Mantle. That moment, I assure you, was as dramatic for me as Babe Ruth "calling his shot" was for another generation of Americans.

Peaks are oftentimes followed by valleys. Mantle struck out on three pitches. Fortunately, though, Yogi Berra was up next, and Yogi lined a three-run triple into right-centerfield to give the Yankees a 6–0 lead. The final score was New York 11, St. Louis 5.

Like the rest of the world, I've grown older since then. For about a dozen years, I was a passionate Yankee fan. Then the thrill wore thin. Still, the magic of that first game remains; and recently, I decided to indulge a whim.

The microfilm room at Columbia University is on the fifth floor of Butler Library. It's a dark, dusty place with countless treasures. But on a sunny spring morning not long ago, there was one particular piece of history I had in mind. I wanted to see what the *New York Times* had to say about an event of unsurpassed importance that had occurred on July 31, 1953.

"The St. Louis Browns," wrote John Drebinger, dean of New York sportswriters, "moved into the stadium yesterday. They stumbled all over themselves, and it wound up with the Yankees romping to an 11 to 5 tri-umph while a gathering of 6,981 fans cheered, laughed, yawned, and drowsed by turns."

Drowsed? Yawned?

Drebinger wasn't paying attention. He got it all wrong. The New York Yankees and St. Louis Browns had just done battle in The Greatest Baseball Game Ever Played.

Two outs; bases loaded; a hated rival . . . It was every boy's dream.

Hero

Sleep-away camp wasn't bad. It's just that I spent most of the summer hoping the place would burn down so I could go home. I was thirteen years old, fat, homesick, and mercilessly picked on. In retrospect, I probably would have picked on me too. The only thing of consequence I could do well was hit a baseball, and that was tempered by my being clumsy and unable to run, field, or throw. So like many boys, I lived vicariously through the exploits of sports heroes.

The year was 1959. Baseball was America's national pastime, and it was an integral part of my life too. I played ball for countless hours after school. Often there were only three of us on a side, and it was necessary to use "imaginary runners." On many occasions, alone in my backyard, I played with imaginary friends. A picture of Babe Ruth's farewell appearance at Yankee Stadium graced my bedroom wall. "You know how bad my voice sounds," the Babe had told sixty-thousand fans that afternoon. He'd been dying of cancer. Everyone knew it, and they hung on his words: "The only real game in the world is baseball."

And now, stuck at Camp Winnebago in the wilds of Maine, baseball was my link to home. During the day, I'd search for a newspaper to scour for box scores. After taps, I'd lie awake in bed, hoping that this would be a night when the weather was just right, the Red Sox would be playing, and I could pick up their games from faraway Boston on my counselor's radio.

It was during those nights as I listened to the radio that Ted Williams rose in my pantheon of gods. 1959 was a bad year for The Splendid Splinter. He was forty years old, and would bat only .254. But the more I learned about his mythic career, the more I felt that, with the possible exception of Babe Ruth, he was the greatest hitter of all time.

Williams made hitting an art and a science. He was even able to estimate that, from the moment a ball leaves the pitcher's hand, the batter has one-tenth of a second to recognize the pitch, another fifteen hundredths of a second to decide whether to swing, and a final fifteen hundredths of a second to do it.

"That's what you're working with," Williams would proclaim. "Four-tenths of a second with a round ball and a round bat." It was his opinion, often voiced, that hitting a baseball was the hardest thing in sports to do.

But the kids at Camp Kennebec always seemed to do it better than the kids at Winnebago. Kennebec was our archrival. It had twice as many campers as we did. They were bigger, tougher; and when it came to inter-camp competition, whatever the sport, Kennebec virtually always won.

Thus, the Winnebago faithful weren't particularly optimistic as they gathered for the annual Kennebec baseball game. We were playing at home. At least, the team would be playing. I was a benchwarmer. And the entire camp would be on our side.

I don't remember much about the first seven-and-a-half innings of the game. I know it was sunny; that Kennebec scored first; that I was rooting hard from the bench; and that Winnebago hung tough. Going into the bottom of the eighth inning, we were behind 7 to 5. The tension mounted as we put a man on base; then another . . . An out; a walk; another out . . . Bases loaded. Two men out. Down by two runs.

Coach Amendola, who had been staring toward the plate, turned toward the bench; it seemed in my direction. I waited. He looked back toward the field again. The on-deck batter moved forward.

"Wait a minute," Coach Amendola said. "I want a pinch-hitter." Then he walked down the bench, stood over me, and said simply, "I'm counting on you, Tom."

And my summer at Camp Winnebago turned golden.

The crowd was hushed as I stepped into the batter's box. Kennebec's pitcher was bigger than I was. He'd been throwing fastballs for most of the afternoon. The outfield was irregularly shaped with a left-field expanse that seemed to go on forever.

The first pitch was a fastball, low and outside.

The bat stayed on my shoulder. "The single most important thing for a hitter is to get a good pitch to hit," Ted Williams once said. "A good hitter can hit a pitch that's over the plate three times better than a great hitter with a ball in a tough spot."

"Ball one," the umpire said.

Second pitch. Fast ball, down the middle.

I swung. Fifty years later, I can still feel the impact of my bat against the ball. There was a loud crack! The ball rocketed toward left-centerfield. And then, from the crowd, there came a roar; the loudest noise I'd ever heard. I wasn't at the Polo Grounds in 1951, but I'm sure it's the sound Bobby Thomson heard. Carlton Fisk must have heard it too in the 1975 World Series. And Kirk Gibson in 1988. The ball landed deep in the gap, and rolled through the grass that stretched forever. Three runners crossed the plate. It would have been four, but I was fat and slow. Discretion being the better part of valor, I stopped at third for a triple. No matter; we were ahead 8 to 7, and I was happier than I'd ever been in my life.

Ted Williams was right: "All great hitters can hit fastballs no matter how fast the pitcher is."

Kennebec went scoreless in the top of the ninth. After the game, "Uncle Howie" came over and hugged me. Uncle Howie owned Camp Winnebago, and had tried for weeks to make me less homesick.

"You're a hero," he told me. "All boys dream about doing what you just did."

Years later, I would run into Uncle Howie at a football game in New York. By then, I had grown to six-foot-three, slimmed down, and become more coordinated. Uncle Howie had no idea who I was. I introduced myself, and a broad smile crossed his face. Then he uttered magic words: "The Kennebec game; you hit a home run with the bases loaded."

"A triple," I corrected. "But it felt like a homer."

And it still does. It always will. Many years later, I had dinner with Reggie Jackson. I was interviewing him for a book I was writing. Toward the end of the meal, Jackson began reminiscing about the three home runs he hit in the final game of the 1977 World Series. "You have no idea how good that felt," he told me.

And all I could think was, "Yes I do, Reggie; I've felt it."

Jerry Izenberg is a joy. It was a pleasure to write this article for and about him.

Jerry Izenberg: An Appreciation

The definitive history of contemporary sports in America has already been written. It starts in 1962 and continues to the present day. It encompasses the rise of the black athlete, westward expansion, the explosion of big money, and the dominance of television. There are vivid portraits of Muhammad Ali, Arnold Palmer, and Bill Russell, and glimpses of Jackie Robinson, Joe Louis, and Babe Ruth. Its author is Jerry Izenberg.

Izenberg's father was born on the Polish-Russian border in a village with no name. It was called "the Jew village." In the early 1890s, when he was eight years old, he and his family walked across half of Europe to get to the sea so they could come to the United States.

Jerry Izenberg was born on September 10, 1930, in Newark, New Jersey. Family legend has it that there was a six-pointed star in the heavens that night.

"My father played semipro baseball and was offered a contract with the New York Giants," Izenberg remembers. "But he turned it down to care for his mother, who was dying. There was also a time when my father fought in illegal smokers with electrician's tape wound around his knuckles which accounted for a high percentage of his knockouts."

"My father loved America," Izenberg continues. "Till the day he died, he told me about being lifted up by his father so he could see the Statue of Liberty as the boat they were on came into New York Harbor. When World War I broke out, he enlisted on the first day. When I got married, he gave me an American flag. His first rule of life was 'work hard,' and he always followed that rule. He worked in a dye-house seven days a week, dying furs. And it killed him. He died of emphysema."

After graduating from high school, Jerry Izenberg enrolled in college at Newark-Rutgers. "I worked forty hours a week at night in a chemical plant to pay for my freshman and sophomore years," he says. "My schedule was classes until noon followed by homework in the library until four o'clock and, after that, work at the factory until midnight. Then the chemical plant blew up and I got two new jobs; one as a short-order cook in a coffee shop and the other as a copy boy for the *Newark Star-Ledger*. Within a month, I was editing everybody else's copy at the paper and had started writing. The more I wrote, the more money I made. After a while, I gave up the job as a short-order cook, much to the relief of everyone in the coffee shop."

Izenberg graduated from college in 1952 and worked at the *Newark Star-Ledger* that summer, writing headlines and high-school sports. "But there was a war going on in Korea," he says. "My father told me, 'You're going to get drafted anyway. Why don't you ask the draft board to move you up on the list and get it over with.' So that's what I did."

After two years in Japan and Korea, Izenberg was discharged from the Army and took a job working for the publisher of three weekly local newspapers in New Jersey. "I was the entire editorial staff," he remembers. "Also the layout designer, photographer, and delivery man." Six months later, he accepted an offer from the *Paterson News*, which was a daily newspaper, at an increase in salary from $65 to $70 dollars a week. "They had me on a split shift five days a week," he remembers. "From 9:00 AM to 2:00 PM and 6:00 PM to 1:00 AM. I did all the sports for them. Then Stanley Woodward entered my life."

Woodward had been sports editor for the *New York Herald Tribune*, where, in Izenberg's words, "he put together the greatest sports staff in the history of journalism." Then he'd had a run-in with management, left the *Tribune*, and taken a job in Miami.

"I read that Woodward was coming to the *Newark Star-Ledger* as an editor," Izenberg says. "So I went to see him. He didn't know who I was, but he talked with me. We had a fairly long conversation and he told me, 'I don't have a job for you now, and I don't know when I'll have one. But I like you; I'll track you.' That year, on Yom Kippur," Izenberg continues, "Woodward called me at home and said, 'I have a job for you. The salary will be $105 a week. Do you think you can work for that?' And I told him, 'I know I can.'"

But Woodward's tenure at the *Star-Ledger* was brief. In 1958, he left the paper and returned to the *New York Herald Tribune*. The following year, his protégé joined him.

"I went because I wanted this man as my mentor," Izenberg explains. "And it was the right decision. The *Herald Tribune* was my school and Stanley Woodward was my professor. Except for my father, he was the most important influence in my life."

Then came a moment of high drama. In 1959, Woodward sent Izenberg to Arizona to cover the San Francisco Giants (who had just left New York) in spring training.

"I thought I was writing good stuff," Izenberg recalls. "And then, in the most humiliating experience of my life, I got a phone call from Stanley one night. He told me, 'I want to see you the day after tomorrow in New York.' So I went back; we met; and he said to me, 'Let me ask you a question. Who's going to play second base for the Giants this year? I don't care about beautiful sunsets. I don't give a fuck about the Painted Desert. I want to know who's going to play second base for the Giants.' And then he chained me to my desk, editing other people's copy for a year."

Finally, in 1960, Izenberg was allowed out into the field again.

"One day," he says, "I looked at the assignment schedule, and I was slated to cover a one-day pro-am golf tournament in Montauk Point. And in case you don't know, Montauk Point is on the tip of Long Island at the edge of the earth. I had to get up at four o'clock in the morning just to get there on time so I could write a 250-word story. Anyway, I defiantly wrote four hundred words instead of 250. And the next day, when I looked in the paper, all four hundred words were there. Then Stanley assigned me to write college basketball, which he hated and thought less of than badminton. But before long, I was getting choice assignments."

Then came another change. In August 1962, the *Newark Star-Ledger* offered Izenberg a job for more money than he was making at the *Tribune*. And they wanted him to write a column.

"You have to take the job," Woodward told him. "It's time you wrote a column. If you don't take it, I'm firing you."

Izenberg has been at the *Newark Star-Ledger* ever since. He now writes four days a week (down from five). His column has been nationally syndicated for four decades and is viewed by many as the best sports journalism ever written.

Izenberg is guided by an uncompromising philosophy of writing.

"When I started work," he says, "there were eight English-language dailies in New York. Many homes in the New York–metropolitan area had three newspapers in them, and newspapers were newspapers. Now journalism is dying. There has been an unforgivable dumbing down in pursuit of advertising revenue, and the entire society is paying for it in nonmonetary ways."

"The business has changed," Izenberg continues. "But I'm not going to change with it. Outside of my family and honesty, the two things that are dearest to my heart are the English language and journalism. My values with regard to writing aren't necessarily current, but they're my values. I'm not the last angry man. There are some people I trust who are under the age of twenty-five. But I believe that, if you're going to kick someone's ass, you have an obligation to tell him first and try to understand his point of view. And I'm tired of what I call 'the razzle-dazzle guys.' Reporters no longer work hard. If something isn't handed to them, they don't bother to write about it. Too many sports writers today are nothing more than paparazzi of the written word. A story breaks; they swarm all over it with little or no understanding; and then they're gone. And you hear all the time, 'Oh, didn't he write a great line.' Well, I don't write great lines. I'm a writer. All the snappy lines in the world can't cover up the absence of a story and a point, which is what a column is about. If you're writing a column, and I write a lot of them, you must do at least one of the following four things: inform, entertain, take a stand, or capture a moment. On my best days, I do all four."

Over the decades, Izenberg has covered virtually every sport and rubbed shoulders with virtually every sports icon of the past fifty years. "Sports at its best is a great thing," he says. "It's who we are. All of us who were alive at the time remember where we were when John Kennedy was shot, when men landed on the moon, when the World Trade Center was attacked. But for a lot of Americans, the preponderance of common unifying memories revolve around sports."

"There's a purity to sports when kids play," Izenberg says, elaborating on his theme. "And there are very few things left in this society that are pure. I love the fact that girls play sports today almost as much as boys; that they share in the experience of representing their school and being part of a team and learn how to condition their bodies. Sports brings out tremendous artistic performances in the face of total adversity. I love watching the better team try to beat the better players. And sports tests character. Working hard; the determination to win fairly and honestly; pushing oneself to the ultimate, both physically and mentally."

"But professional sports are now out of control," Izenberg proclaims. "The Olympics symbolize it best. The International, Olympic Committee is nothing but a five-ringed Mafia. They're the worst, most corrupt, self-serving thugs in the world. Everything from choosing a site to judging the individual athletic competitions is marked by intimidation and corruption. The Olympics offer inspiring performances and moments of great personal drama. But the Olympic Games as a whole are a sham and a fraud."

"I love baseball," Izenberg continues. "That's why I go to as many Minor League games as possible. Baseball is the greatest traditional sport in the world, but the people who run Major League Baseball today are ruining the game. Baseball has great athletes; but more importantly, it's a mood, a tradition. And that tradition is being lost as we speak. My father took me the Polo Grounds when I was twelve years old. It was the Giants against the Dodgers. Carl Hubbell was pitching. Hubbell was forty years old and his arm was shot, but it was the war and ballplayers were in short supply. I remember my father telling me that afternoon, 'Pay attention, because one day you'll remember that you saw this man pitch.' For six innings, Hubbell pitched well; although he was pitching with his head, not his arm. Then, in the seventh inning, he got shellacked. Mel Ott, who was the Giants' manager, took him out. The fans gave him a standing ovation that I still remember. But go to a Major League Baseball game now and it's almost impossible to talk with the person sitting next to you. The sound system is at a decibel level that would shatter every stained glass window in the Notre Dame Cathedral. Everything is hype, advertising on uniforms, Spiderman on the bases. And the rocket scientists behind it all say, 'We're bringing excitement to the game.' Gee, I'm stupid. I thought excitement was the Yankees versus the Red Sox. I thought excitement was Randy Johnson throwing a perfect game at age forty."

"Look at today's athletes," Izenberg says, shifting gears. "There are athletes who do wonderful things with their fame and fortune. David Robinson is unbelievable. And there are lesser-known guys like Bob

Ojeda and Al Leiter, who are incredibly generous with their time and money. Gary Carter's mother died of leukemia, and I've never known an athlete who was more involved in a charitable cause than Gary Carter is in fighting leukemia. Arthur Ashe and Ted Williams were terrific. So was Muhammad Ali. But what does that say about the others, who are making enough money to air-condition hell but don't do anything for anybody but themselves."

Now Izenberg is on a roll. "Then there's drugs," he says. "I don't know if Barry Bonds and Sammy Sosa are on steroids or not, although I do know that what happened to their bodies over the years looks very strange to me. And I know that this is an area where sports is corrupting society. People say, if they want to cheat, let them do it. But the people who say that never looked into Lyle Alzado's eyes when he was dying, and I did. And what bothers me most is that there's now a crisis in America's high schools with regard to steroid use. More and more young people, boys and girls, are using performance-enhancing drugs to compete. So as far as the steroid-using pill-popping role models are concerned; let their dicks fall off, let their kidneys die, and may the women go childless."

Izenberg's artistry hasn't been limited to the newspaper business. He created and was on camera for a Sunday-night television show called *Sports Extra* that ran for eight years in the 1970s. In the 1980s, he hosted a two-hour issue-oriented Sunday-night radio show on the NBC network. He has produced, directed, written, and/or narrated close to fifty television documentaries. And he has authored nine books.

On the home front, Izenberg has been married three times. He describes his first wife, to whom he was married for nineteen years, as "the beast from twenty thousand fathoms." His second marriage, which lasted for five years, was to "a very nice woman, but the marriage was a mistake. That was my fault."

Wife number three is Aileen Izenberg, who served as a teacher and administrator in the Newark school system for thirty-three years. She and Jerry have been married since 1978. Putting their families together, they have four children and seven grandchildren with another grandchild on the way.

Politically, Izenberg is something of an anomaly. He was once a member of the Communist Party, and after that, the Socialist Labor Party. He worked for Adlai Stevenson in the 1950s and "once flirted with the

Republican Party." But in his words, "Right now, I have no political party. I can't find one that meets my prerequisites, which are a belief in human dignity, a belief in individual rights, a belief that individuals should be held responsible for their conduct, and an aversion to trying to get over on the system for personal or political gain."

"My family, my work, and my country are important to me," Izenberg says, expounding upon his values. "I love this country; but America can be very unfair and cruel, and I spend a lot of time thinking about how to make it better. That's what Project Pride is about."

Project Pride is an undertaking that is dear to Izenberg's heart and a persistent never-ending demand upon his time.

Twenty-five years ago, several civic leaders in Newark got a $1,500 grant from the Chamber of Commerce to remove graffiti. They came to Izenberg to ask for help in raising $500 more. From that kernel of hope, Project Pride was born.

Project Pride offers inner-city students in Newark a variety of classes in reading, science, and computer studies as well as SAT preparation courses, music lessons, and other after-school programs. It has generated college scholarships in amounts as high as $10,000 for 931 students. Its alumni include doctors, lawyers, teachers, and scientists.

At its peak, Project Pride had an annual budget of $220,000 and worked with 3,000 students a year. Now, because of limited funds, those numbers are down to $160,000 and 1,500. "People are giving less," Izenberg notes. "And we're in competition with a large number of poverty pimps who deliver nothing."

The centerpiece of Project Pride's fund raising is the "Pride Bowl" football game held each year in October.

The first Pride Bowl was contested in 1979.

"It was a total nightmare," Izenberg acknowledges. "I'm a sports-writer, a critic. And all of a sudden, I found myself as a promoter, which was when I began to understand what people who put on sports events go through. The game was between Seton Hall and Cheyney State. It rained the entire week. The public-transit company refused to add additional buses to the route for the game."

"Now it's the day of the game," Izenberg reports, continuing down memory lane. "Little kids from local schools are holding up placards with letters on them to spell out cheers, but the kids are standing in the wrong order so the letters are spelling out gibberish. I have parolees from a halfway house blowing up red and blue balloons, but the balloons don't have enough helium in them so they won't lift up. The guy who is supposed to give the signal for the two teams to run out onto the field is having an epileptic fit and is lying on the ground . . ."

This year's game (the twenty-sixth Pride Bowl) will take place at Newark Riverfront Stadium. The Army and Navy lightweight football squads will face off against each other.

"Over the years," says Izenberg, "the most memorable thing about the games has been what the players take away from them. Each team is adopted by a local high school. The kids from the school interact with the players and some interesting bonds are formed."

Meanwhile, it can be honestly said that Jerry Izenberg is a treasure; a wonderful writer, an engaging story teller, and an arbiter of values. He should have won the Pulitzer Prize for Commentary long ago. But the jury that designates Pulitzer winners is journalism's answer to boxing's world sanctioning organizations with the *New York Times* playing the role of Don King.

If we're lucky, Izenberg will write his memoirs some day. But that would be the crib notes version. To fully appreciate his work, one has to have read his columns; day after day, week after week, year after year. Ten thousand columns crafted over the span of more than four decades. Indeed, if the *Newark Star-Ledger* is interested in performing a true public service, it will assemble those columns in multi-volume sets, put the sets in major libraries across the country, and give Izenberg a set to take home with him.

Izenberg knows he's good at what he does. Most superstars do. But he also acknowledges the debt he owes to others. "I've been fortunate," he says, "in that, over the years, I've learned a lot from a lot of great writers. Stanley Woodward taught me integrity. Tommy Holmes taught me that, whether you love them or hate them, you have to care about the people you write about. From Red Smith, I got permission to use the English language. From Jimmy Cannon, I learned how to hear as a New Yorker. I could go on. Jesse Abramson, Al Laney, Joe Palmer . . ."

Today's writers could learn a lot by reading Jerry Izenberg.

Bill Bradley is my idea of what a public servant should be. But like millions of Americans, I knew him first as a basketball player.

Bill Bradley Remembered

The first time I saw Bill Bradley, I was a freshman at Columbia and he was a junior at Princeton. It was Saturday night, January 18, 1964, at Columbia's antiquated University Gymnasium. The Lions had an ordinary team, but a sell-out crowd of 2,050 had gathered.

Despite being only twenty years old, Bradley had captivated the nation. He was the best college basketball player in the country, multitalented and intensely handsome. Even then, people spoke of him as a future president of the United States. John McPhee had begun to research a profile of him for publication in *The New Yorker.*

It was an electric night. Bradley played the game differently from the other players, like a grown man among children. But unlike later Princeton teams, this one had a weak supporting cast. Columbia executed close to perfection and took a 31–19 halftime lead. Princeton rallied to tie the score at 47, but the Lions hung tough and won 69–66. Bradley scored 36 points. No one else for Princeton managed double figures. It was a sweet victory for the Lions against their most hated rival.

Eleven months later, Bradley was in New York again; this time for the Holiday Festival at Madison Square Garden. Back then, the Holiday Festival was the most important midseason basketball tournament in the nation. In December 1964, it offered a classic confrontation between Princeton and the top-ranked representative of big time college basketball—#1 Michigan.

On the Columbia campus, distaste for Princeton was balanced by the belief that a good showing by the Tigers against Michigan would be a plus for the Ivy League as a whole and hence for Columbia. After all, Bradley represented not just Princeton but the entire Ivy League philosophy. Bradley dominated the Wolverines, scoring 41 points before fouling out with Princeton ahead by twelve markers. The Garden crowd gave him a three-minute standing ovation. There were four minutes, thirty-seven seconds left in the game. And Princeton folded, losing by four points.

Still, the Bill Bradley legend was growing. He was a banker's son from Crystal City, Missouri, who had chosen the Ivy League over big-time college basketball. Despite being double- and triple-teamed, he led the nation in scoring his senior year of college, averaging 32.3 points per game. Ultimately, he would finish his college career with 2,503 points, placing him third in the record book at that time behind Oscar Robertson and Frank Selvy. Classically graceful on and off the court, he was a scholar-athlete in every sense of the word. After his final home game at Princeton, his classmates, with the permission of the school administration, presented him with the cast-iron clapper from the bell in Nassau Hall. Nassau Hall was the oldest building on the Princeton campus. The bell had sounded every day dating back to a time before the American Revolution.

The capstone of Bradley's college basketball career was the 1965 NCAA Tournament. Princeton beat Penn State and North Carolina State before facing Providence in the regional finals. The Friars had lost only once all season and were heavily favored. But Princeton had Bradley. "A Whole Team Touched by Stardust" was how *Sports Illustrated* headlined its account of the Tigers' stunning 109–69 upset victory.

That put Princeton in the Final Four for a rematch against Michigan. Once again, Princeton took the lead; this time by five points. And once again, several questionable calls put Bradley in foul trouble. With their star on the bench, the Tigers faltered. Michigan pulled away and won by seventeen.

But Bradley's career wasn't over. Two nights later, against Wichita State in the consolation game to decide third place, he erupted for 58 points to set an NCAA-tournament single-game scoring record. Now, without doubt, Bill Bradley was "our guy"—a belief that was confirmed three years later.

After graduating from college, Bradley spent two years as a Rhodes Scholar and six months on active duty with the United States Air Force Reserve. Then he joined the New York Knicks.

Meanwhile, on a cold winter night in February 1968, Columbia was readying to play Princeton at University Gymnasium. Just before the opening tip-off, Bill Bradley walked into the gym. Several students noticed him and began to applaud. Heads turned and more spectators applauded. Soon, virtually every person in Columbia's home arena was standing in a sustained ovation.

That tribute occurred more than three decades ago. But the memory of it has been on my mind now that Bradley has formed a presidential exploratory committee and begun the process of raising funds to run for president in the year 2000.

"Bill Bradley is too dull," people tell us. "He's not charismatic enough. He talks too slowly."

But there's something very reassuring about Bill Bradley. He's a decent, honorable, thoughtful man. He was always more than a basketball player, and now he's more than a politician. If the American people are smart, they'll grab him.

I got to know Wilt Chamberlain through my association with Muhammad Ali.

Wilt Chamberlain (1936–1999)

As Jerry West recently observed, "Wilt Chamberlain was one of those fabulous players who defined sports."

Chamberlain entered the NBA in 1959, and changed the way the game was played with his unique combination of size, agility, and strength. He was the league's dominant player for fourteen years; first with the Philadelphia Warriors (who later moved to San Francisco); then with the Philadelphia 76ers and Los Angeles Lakers. Along the way, he rewrote the record book like no athlete in any sport ever has.

When Chamberlain entered the NBA in 1959, the league record for points in a single season was 2,105. As a rookie, Wilt scored 2,707. In his third season, he raised the standard to 4,029 and averaged 50.4 points per game. He led the NBA in scoring in each of his first seven campaigns, during which he averaged 39.6 points per contest. To put that number in perspective, no one else in NBA history has averaged more than 37.1 points per game over the course of a season.

When Chamberlain entered the league, the best single-season field-goal percentage ever was .490. Wilt's rookie mark was .509. In 1972–73, he shot a staggering .727 from the floor. He led the league in field-goal percentage nine times and once made 35 consecutive field goals in NBA play. His Achilles heel, of course, was free-throw shooting. Over the course of his career, Chamberlain registered a mediocre .511 from the charity line. Yet ironically, he also holds the record for the most free throws ever in an NBA game. That occurred in Hershey, Pennsylvania, on the night of March 2, 1962, when he converted on 28 of 32 foul shots en route to scoring 100 points against the New York Knicks; the most points ever scored in an NBA contest.

When Chamberlain entered the league, Bill Russell held the single-season NBA record for rebounds with 1,612. As a rookie, Wilt pulled down 1,941. One year later, he raised the standard to 2,149. The top seven rebounding seasons in NBA history belong to Wilt Chamberlain. He led the NBA in rebounding eleven times. He also leads the league in career rebounding with 23,924. He once had 55 rebounds in a single game and averaged 22.9 rebounds per game throughout his career. Again, to put that number in perspective, over the course of his career, Kareem Abdul-Jabbar averaged 11.4 rebounds per game.

In 1967–68, Chamberlain was the only center ever to lead the league in assists. He once averaged 48.5 minutes per game for an entire season. That's four full quarters plus a bit of overtime per game. Chamberlain averaged 45.8 minutes per game throughout his career. He once played 47 consecutive complete games.

And oh yes; he never fouled out of an NBA contest.

In fourteen seasons, Chamberlain's teams made the playoffs thirteen times. They played for the NBA championship on six occasions, winning twice. Two of those championship losses were to the Boston Celtics, who also defeated Chamberlain-led teams in the conference finals five times. His rivalry with Bill Russell stands as history's greatest personal rivalry within a team sport.

Moreover, Chamberlain's athletic prowess wasn't limited to basketball. He was a magnificent track-and-field competitor. He was perhaps the finest volleyball player ever. And beyond that, for a brief period in 1971, he was at the vortex of professional boxing. In fact, in early 1971, Wilt and Muhammad Ali actually signed a contract to fight one another. But then Ali lost to Joe Frazier and the contract had to be renegotiated.

"I took it seriously," Chamberlain later recalled. "I spent some time training with Cus D'Amato. I believed I was capable of going out there and representing myself in a way that would not be embarrassing. I thought I could acquit myself reasonably well. I didn't have to learn how to become a complete boxer. I was going to learn for eight or ten months how to apply my strengths and skills against one person. One of the first things Cus said to me was, 'You're going to learn how to fight one man; that's all. We're going to have all the tapes of Ali. We're going to know all the things you have to do and what you possess to do it with against this one person. There's no way that Ali can train to fight you. He won't know anything about you as a fighter because there's only one of you and no tapes.'"

"That was my edge," Chamberlain continued. "Ali would be coming in blind. He'd have no idea what he was facing, whereas I'd know what to expect. And of course, I had God-given strength, size, and athletic ability. If I'd been the odds-maker, I'd have made Muhammad a ten-to-one favorite. But I thought a man as great at his job as Ali was might take me lightly. I could see that happening. And because of his nature, he'd want to have fun with this particular fight, which might give me an opening. I truly believed there was a chance for me to throw one punch and take Ali out."

Ultimately, the fight never took place. Chamberlain said that renegotiations failed over economic issues. Ali's promoter, Bob Arum, claimed that Wilt simply chickened out. Bill Russell offered what was perhaps the best epitaph for the bout when he said simply, "I can't speak for Wilt. I just know that I personally would never challenge a champion in his field of expertise. I would never get in a boxing ring with Ali or on the football field with Jim Brown or on a track with Carl Lewis. I would never impose my thoughts or motivations on someone else. But for me personally, that's just not the way I am."

But it was the way Wilt was. The title of his 1973 autobiography—*Wilt: Just Like Any Other 7-Foot Black Millionaire Who Lives Next Door*—said it all. Wilt was different. His thoughts often ran against the grain, and he spoke his mind regardless of whether or not his views were popular. He even had the temerity to challenge the prevailing view that Muhammad Ali in the 1960s was a spokesman for black America.

"I knew Muhammad fairly well during his time of glory," Chamberlain once declared. "I liked the man; I still do. And I applauded some of the stands he took; for example, his refusal to go into the war. But when Muhammad was held up as a spokesman for black people, I thought that was ludicrous because Muhammad was a guy writing lightweight poetry who happened to be a tremendous athlete, who was not educated in areas where somebody who speaks for a group of people should be. If somebody like Muhammad was speaking for black America, then black America was in bad shape."

Wilt Chamberlain was so strong and so physically gifted that at times he seemed imperious to the physical afflictions that beset lesser men. To see the life leave such a physically imposing figure so prematurely reminds all of us that we are mortal. Meanwhile, athletes around the world are in mourning with the words, "We'll miss you, brother."

A boxing website headquartered in England was an unusual place to write about an American baseball player. But that was my forum when Ted Williams died.

Ted Williams
(1918–2002)

The fraternity of great athletes transcends any one particular sport. The death of one is felt by all. Death is a reminder that, no matter how young and strong an athlete might be, the body that serves as a vehicle to glory will ultimately fail.

Ted Williams was a great athlete. That's the first thing to be said about him. By most reckonings, he was the greatest pure hitter of all time. Five men in the history of Major League Baseball had a higher batting average. Others hit more home runs. But no one combined the two like Williams did.

The world has grown accustomed to books "by" athletes. Invariably, these books are written "with" someone else. Often, the athlete never reads his book. He simply talks into a tape recorder, answering questions for a day or two. Then the real author fills in the rest from press clippings. When Ted Williams finally got around to writing a book, he worked with John Underwood but the end product was vintage Williams.

The Science of Hitting, published in 1970, remains the classic work on hitting a baseball. Among the thoughts Williams offered were:

★ "All they ever write about the great hitters is what great reflexes they have, what great style, what strength, what quickness; but never how smart the guy is at the plate, and that's fifty percent of it."

★ "I was known as a hitter who guessed a lot. But for me, guessing was observing."

★ "The single most important thing for a hitter is to get a good pitch to hit. A good hitter can hit a pitch that's over the plate three times better than a great hitter with a ball in a tough spot."

★ "If a pitcher is throwing fast balls and curves and only the fast balls are in the strike zone, you'd be silly to look for a curve, wouldn't you?"

★ "My preference was a light bat [33 ounces]. When we started using pine tar or resin and oil on the handles to improve the grip, I cleaned my bats with alcohol every night. I took them to the post office to check their weights. Finally, I got the Red Sox to put a scale in the clubhouse. I wanted them checked because bats pick up condensation and dirt being on the ground. They can gain an ounce or more in a surprisingly short time."

Williams came up to the major leagues as a twenty-year-old prodigy in 1939 when baseball was truly the national pastime and the sport was deeply ingrained in the fabric of America. When he first donned a Boston Red Sox uniform (the only one he wore during his career), Lou Gehrig and Carl Hubbel were still active players. He retired in 1960, having played through three revolutions that changed the game—the advent of television, the arrival of Jackie Robinson, and westward expansion.

His records stand as a testament to his prowess. Despite losing three full seasons (1943–1945) in his prime to serve as a Navy pilot in World War II and two more (1952–1953) as a Marine pilot during the Korean War, he played up to a standard that today's hitters can only dream about.

"The days pile one on another to make a career," Williams once said. And what a career it was! 521 home runs . . . 2,654 hits . . . 1,839 RBIs . . . 1,798 runs . . . 2,161 walks . . . a slugging percentage of .690 . . . an on-base percentage of .483 (the highest ever) . . . and a .344 career batting average (unequaled since his day).

Along the way, Williams won six batting titles and led the league in home runs four times, runs scored six times, RBIs four times, walks eight times, slugging percentage eight times, and on-base percentage twelve times. He won two triple crowns, was voted the American League's most valuable player twice, and was chosen as an All-Star on sixteen occasions (all but his rookie season and the years he missed because of military service). In 1957, at age thirty-nine, he became the oldest man to win a batting title in either league. He won the batting crown again at age forty. If World War II and Korea hadn't intervened, his accomplishments would have been even more formidable.

Williams was also the last man to bat .400 for an entire season. The way he did it shed light on his character.

In 1941 (Williams's third year in the major leagues) his average stood at .39955 going into the final day of the season. Because of the manner in which baseball keeps statistics, that number would have been rounded off to .400. Red Sox manager Joe Cronin offered to let him sit out a double-header against the Philadelphia Athletics. But Williams insisted on playing that day and got six hits in eight at bats to raise his average to .406.

That's a champion.

"No hitter has it all," Williams later wrote. "There probably never has been what you would call the complete hitter. Babe Ruth struck out more than he should have. Ty Cobb didn't have power."

But Ted Williams had it all. When Pete Rose was chasing the immortal Cobb's record of 4,191 career base hits, Rose opined, "No one can tell me that Ty Cobb would have hit .367 if he started playing ball in 1963. Don't even figure in night ball and relief pitchers. Just look at the gloves the players had back then; short fingers held together at the end by rawhide." Then Rose added, "But Ted Williams could have hit .344 in any era."

Williams was more than a great hitter. He was also a humanitarian. His work on behalf of various charities made the efforts of his contemporaries in sports pale by comparison. And when he was inducted into the Baseball Hall of Fame in 1966, he used the occasion to voice the view, "I hope that some day Satchel Paige and Josh Gibson will be voted into the Hall of Fame as symbols of the great Negro players who are not here only because they weren't given the chance."

Five years later, Satchel Paige was inducted at Cooperstown. Gibson and other greats from the Negro League followed.

Williams also had a soft spot in his heart for boxing. "I feel the greatest prize in sports is the heavyweight championship of the world," he said. "I happen to have been successful in baseball, but if you want to talk about dedication, take a fighter who climbs to the top and stays there."

Williams placed Joe Louis at the top of his rankings. "I think that Joe Louis was the greatest heavyweight fighter who ever lived," he reminisced. "I loved his style, his punch, his aggressiveness. He was moving in all the time; stalking you, stalking you. He fought everybody. He fought more often than anybody. To me, nobody will be a greater heavyweight than Joe Louis."

But Williams also spoke fondly of Muhammad Ali. "As for Vietnam and the political side of things," he said during an interview in 1989, "I served in two wars as a pilot. My career was interrupted several times, and I didn't agree with what Ali did, but I respected him for it. Ali's faith was important to him. He was sincere and he acted in accord with his convictions."

"I have great admiration for Ali," Williams continued. "My first experience meeting him came [in 1966] at the airport in Tampa. I saw him from quite a distance, maybe two hundred feet. Ali looked in my direction, and apparently he recognized me because he started to walk toward me. He got right up to me. I don't remember exactly how he said it, but the gist of it was, 'I'm Muhammad Ali.' I said, 'I know who you are,' and we started talking. He was going to Canada to fight George Chuvalo. And he told me, 'Chuvalo's a tough guy, but I won't have any trouble with him.' I always admired his confidence; saying he was going to do something and then, by God, going out and doing it."

"Ali was absolutely devoted to being the best, and he was one of the greatest fighters who ever lived," Williams said in closing. "I've seen him fight live; I've seen all his films. What always amazes me is the way he maneuvered in the ring. There's no question in my mind that he was the fastest big man ever in boxing. And I think he got as much out of his physical ability as possible, which is another reason I admire him. He came as close as any athlete I know to getting the most out of his potential. I've been a fan of his for a long, long time."

Ali, for his part, responded in kind, saying simply, "Ted Williams was as great in his sport as I was in mine."

*Writing Howard Cosell's obituary presented the problem of how to rec-
oncile the man's enormous contribution to sports journalism with his
lesser side.*

Howard Cosell
(1918–1995)

When The Grim Reaper comes, it's best to speak well of the
departed. So let it be said first that Howard Cosell changed the face of
sports commentary in America. There were talented broadcasters before
him, but Cosell brought something new to the game—a willingness to
speak the truth in hard situations. That was particularly evident in the
1960s, when Cassius Clay changed his name to Muhammad Ali and
refused induction into the United States Army. Cosell wasn't Ali's only
defender. Writers like Jerry Izenberg and Robert Lipsyte were equally
eloquent in support of Muhammad's cause. But Cosell had access to television; an extraordinarily powerful new medium. And because of that, his
name will be linked with Ali's forever.

There was also a time when Howard Cosell was good for boxing.
Like him or not, he had the most recognizable voice in America and was
boxing's only nationally known commentator. He had the ability to go
before a major sports audience, and by virtue of his presence, make almost
any event seem important. For two decades, he was integral to the sport.
Then, in 1982, he walked away, telling an interviewer, "I now favor the
abolition of professional boxing. It's utterly immoral; it's not capable of
reformation. You'll never clean it up. Mud can never be clean."

That, of course, was Cosell's prerogative. Just as he urged others, particularly black athletes, to speak their mind, he also had First Amendment
rights. But something beyond the Constitution always seemed to be pushing Howard Cosell on. Ultimately, he began to act as though he was more
important than the events he covered. Despite an enormously successful
career, he became an increasingly bitter and abusive man.

My own first contact with Cosell was a positive experience. It came in 1962. I was a high-school junior. He was hosting pre- and post-game radio shows for the New York Mets. I wrote him a letter suggesting that he was becoming a "shill." I doubt very much that an eleventh grader ever caused more consternation at ABC. Several days later, when I got home from school, my mother told me, "Someone named Howard Cosell called this morning." The next day, I received a typed two-page single-spaced letter in the mail.

"Dear Tom," the missive began. "Despite a flood of mail, I am answering your letter as immediately as I have received it for one very important reason—I respect it." (The man wrote like he talked.) The letter went on to reaffirm Cosell's commitment to truth, and closed with the words, "I shall not change; I assure you of that. I have gone my way regardless of the fact that much of the public seems to prefer bland tripe to forthright exposition, and I shall continue to do so. Meanwhile, I ask that you, as an intelligent listener, bear in mind that life is complex, integrity is precious, and that working before and after the Mets games has been the biggest challenge to my courage—as a married man with children—that I have ever faced."

That was my introduction to Howard Cosell. We met face-to-face twenty-two years later when I was researching a book entitled *The Black Lights*. I went to ABC for an interview, and was ushered into "The Great One's" office. He was on the telephone with Eddie Einhorn, who owned the Chicago White Sox. The first words I heard him say were, "Eddie; take your fucking ball club and shove it up your ass." Then the conversation got ugly.

Five years later, while researching *Muhammad Ali: His Life And Times*, I had occasion to interview Cosell again. Another time, I was a guest on his radio talk show, "Speaking Of Everything." He invited me both to the Friars Club and to his home. But it really wasn't worth the price, because the cost of access was nonstop abuse; of me, of the people he worked with, of the world at large. I mean, how can you digest your lunch when you're sitting next to someone who's saying, "Alex Wallau has cancer, and he deserves it."

The last time I saw Howard Cosell was at CORE's annual Martin Luther King Day dinner in 1992. Secretary of State James Baker and Muhammad Ali were the guests of honor. The schedule called for Cosell to make a presentation, after which I would introduce Ali. I arrived at the pre-dinner reception with Ali, saw Cosell sitting alone, and went over to shake hands with him.

"How are you, sir?"

All I got in return was an icy stare followed by the words, "How dare they ruin my presentation by asking the likes of you to introduce Muhammad Ali?"

That was the last time I saw Howard Cosell. So yes, he was important. And yes, he did some very good things. I just wish he had been nicer about it all.

No sports commentator in America ever had more detractors than Howard Cosell; and none was more respected. Such a man deserves critics no less forthright than he was.

Arthur Ashe was a graceful man in both his professional and personal life.

Arthur Ashe
(1943–1993)

Riddick Bowe knocked out Michael Dokes at Madison Square Garden last night (February 6, 1993). Years from now, what I'll remember most about the evening is a moment of shared grief. Shortly before the bout began, it was announced that Arthur Ashe had died.

There was a moan of collective sorrow from the crowd. A good man has been taken from us long before what should have been his time.

Ashe rose to prominence as the first black superstar in men's tennis. He's the only black man to win the men's singles title at the U.S. Open (1965), Australian Open (1970), or Wimbledon (1975). He underwent a quadruple bypass surgery after suffering a heart attack in 1979 and retired from competitive tennis a year later.

Arthur lived a full life after he left the playing field. He was a devoted husband and father. On the professional side of the ledger, he authored an autobiography and *A Hard Road To Glory* (a three-volume history of the African American athlete); served as president of Artists and Athletes Against Apartheid and captain of the U.S. Davis Cup team; worked as a sports commentator for ABC and HBO; and was deeply involved in a number of charitable causes. Last year, he founded the Arthur Ashe Institute for Urban Health. In December, *Sports Illustrated* designated him as its Sportsman of the Year.

I met Arthur on three occasions. The first was when I interviewed him at his apartment in Manhattan in 1989 for a book that I was writing; *Muhammad Ali: His Life and Times.*

Ashe was critical of certain aspects of Ali's life.

"I never went along with the pronouncements of Elijah Muhammad [Ali's spiritual leader when he joined the Nation of Islam]," Arthur told me. "It was a racist ideology, a sort of American apartheid, and I didn't like it. But Ali combined his athletic talent with social action during the

1960s, when both he and the black social revolution reached their peak. And the result was that he became an icon for literally millions of black Americans."

"I personally can remember feeling all tingly when Ali refused to step forward at that induction center in Houston in 1967," Ashe added. "It wasn't just that he'd lose his title. I thought the man was going to jail. I really believe that, if Ali hadn't done what he did, Harry Edwards wouldn't have gotten a fraction of the support he got in 1968 to boycott the Mexico City Olympics. I know Ali certainly influenced me later in 1967. The Davis Cup draw came up; and lo and behold, the United States was supposed to meet South Africa in the third round. I was thinking to myself, 'Oh, my God. Just three months ago, Muhammad Ali refused to cross the line. And here I am, the only black player in tennis, the main member of the Davis Cup team.' There's no question that Ali's sacrifice was in the forefront of my mind. Fortunately, the president of the United States Tennis Association then was Robert Kelleher, a wonderful man. We talked about it, and he suggested that the most effective way to deal with the situation would be for us to give up the home-court advantage. We had what was known as choice of ground. Kelleher told me, 'Let's do something that has never been done in the history of Davis Cup competition. Let's offer to play South Africa in South Africa and go down there and beat the crap out of them. Let South Africa see a black person win in their own backyard. It never came to that. South Africa lost to West Germany in the second round. But Ali was very much in my thoughts."

Two years later, I sat with Arthur for a second time. I was speaking with a cross section of black leadership in America for a twenty-two-page feature that would appear in *Penthouse* magazine. Arthur was one of eight people I interviewed, along with Jesse Jackson, John Lewis, Charles Rangel, Mary Francis Berry, Roger Wilkins, Sterling Johnson, and Harry Belafonte.

We talked about the role of sports in breaking down racial barriers. Then I asked, "What sort of moral obligation do you think today's African American athletes have?"

"That's the central question," Arthur told me. "I believe they have a moral obligation to assist, and don't just assist blacks. It's a play off the adage, 'From those to whom much has been given, much is expected.' If you're doing that well, there is definitely a role that you can play to help the situation. If you don't do it, I think that's a serious omission."

"The athletes today," Ashe continued, "very few of them seem to have a moral or historical consciousness about how they got to where they are. The most famous statement that is bandied about now is the one that Vince Coleman made. Major League Baseball was celebrating Jackie Robinson's fortieth anniversary. Vince Coleman was asked, 'What did Jackie Robinson mean to you?' And Vince Coleman's answer was, 'I don't know nothing about no Jackie Robinson.' It was said in a way that meant, 'Don't bother me; that stuff doesn't matter to me; I could care less who Jackie Robinson was.' It was almost like, 'All I care about is doing as well as I can, so I can make as much money as I can.' And I say it has gone too far. It's okay to be an individualist if you're responsible. But some of these athletes, black athletes, don't want to be role models. They are loath to speak up about social issues. It's like pulling teeth to get them to show up at some political function or fundraiser. I'm not saying that it's true of all of them, but it's very difficult. You would not have had to do that with Jackie Robinson or Wilt Chamberlain or Jim Brown. This generation just seems to be out for themselves, although obviously there are some exceptions."

Last summer, I crossed paths with Ashe one last time. I was in New Jersey with Muhammad Ali for a fundraiser to benefit Project Pride.

Arthur had just announced that had AIDS. In 1983, he'd undergone a second heart operation. Five years later, he learned that he was HIV-positive as a consequence of a blood transfusion received during the second surgery. He'd kept his illness private until he learned that *USA Today* was on the verge of publishing an article about his condition.

The dinner began with a reception in Ali's honor. Muhammad was seated in a cushioned chair in a room adjacent to the banquet hall. He has reached a time in his life when it can be difficult for him to interact with crowds. I'd been asked to sit beside him to keep the reception line moving and ensure that things went smoothly.

It was a long line. People waited patiently for their moment with The Greatest . . . A handshake, an autograph, a photo, words of adoration . . . Then the person talking with Muhammad would move on as another moved into place.

At one point, I looked toward the far end of the room to see how many more people were in line. Arthur Ashe was standing near the end of the line, patiently waiting his turn.

No pulling rank . . . No "I'm a famous celebrity" . . .

I stood up and walked over to Arthur.

"You shouldn't be here," I told him. "You should be sitting with Muhammad."

I brought Ashe to the head of the line. Muhammad rose and embraced him.

They sat together for the rest of the reception.

That's the image of Arthur that I'll always carry with me. Arthur Ashe and Muhammad Ali, side-by-side. Two giants of our time.

*Marvin Miller deserves to be enshrined in the Baseball Hall of Fame.
But like the people who have conspired to deny him his due, I have less
than fond memories of him.*

Are Baseball Ballplayers Happy?:
A Personal Memory of Marvin Miller

Marvin Miller is a towering figure in sports history. In 1966, when he
was elected executive director the Major League Baseball Players
Association, players were bound to their club by a "reserve clause" that
precluded free negotiation. Pensions were negligible. Most labor issues
were resolved by club owners in a dictatorial manner.

In 1968, Miller negotiated the first collective-bargaining agreement
in the history of professional sports. The agreement raised baseball's annual
minimum salary from $6,000 to $10,000. More significantly, it began the
process of laying a foundation for an effective labor movement. The tide
turned irrevocably in 1975, when an arbitrator (and later, the federal
courts) upheld a challenge to baseball's reserve clause. Free agency for
players with six years' service in the major leagues was incorporated into
the next collective bargaining agreement. In 1970, the average salary for
a major league baseball player was $29,303. By 2006, that number had
increased almost one-hundred-fold to $2,866,544.

Miller's creation became the standard that other sports unions aspire
to. He formally stepped down as executive director of the MLBPA in late
1982. One of his last acts of leadership was mean-spirited and destructive.
I know, because I was on the receiving end of it. And I think it constituted
a disservice to the players he served so effectively for most of his reign.

Let me explain.

As a child, I was a passionate baseball fan. I went to doubleheaders
regularly at Yankee Stadium and knew the names of virtually every player
in the major leagues.

Fast forward to 1982. I was thirty-six years old. Five year earlier, I'd
left my job as a litigator with a prominent Wall Street law firm to pursue

a career as a writer. My first book (*Missing*) had served as the basis for the Academy Award–winning film starring Jack Lemmon and Sissy Spacek. Two novels and another non-fiction book followed. Boxing writing was an unimagined part of my future. I was no longer a passionate baseball fan, but still followed the sport with interest.

Baseball in 1982 was in a state of transition. A 1981 strike had led to the cancellation of 706 games (38 percent of the season) and engendered considerable public resentment toward the players. Times are different now. The public is used to astronomical salaries for athletes. But in 1982, $241,497 (the average player salary) struck many as an exorbitant amount of money for "playing a game."

I had a friend (a professor of psychiatry named Bill Hoffmann) who dabbled in sports psychology. Bill and I were of the view that a baseball player's life was harder than it seemed. But could we quantify that notion?

In September 1982, Dr. Hoffmann and I proposed an article to *Sports Illustrated*. The first paragraph of our proposal read, "Countless articles have been written about what makes professional athletes win, but little has been said about what makes them happy. The popular perception is that ballplayers have a great life—good pay, lots of adulation; they don't even 'work' for a living. But scratch the veneer of a professional athlete and two demons surface: fear of failure and the fear of growing old."

We then proposed putting together a psychological testing questionnaire and sending it to every member of the Major League Baseball Players Association as the foundation of our research, analyzing the results, conducting follow-up interviews with players, and writing about our findings.

Sports Illustrated found the idea intriguing and asked us to prepare a draft questionnaire. If it was satisfactory, the magazine would pay the cost of copying and postage. Once the data was in, *SI* would decide whether or not it wanted to commission the article. If it didn't, Dr. Hoffmann and I would be free to sell our work elsewhere.

At that point, I telephoned the Major League Baseball Players Association and was referred to Peter Rose (associate general counsel for the organization). I asked him if the MLBPA would cooperate by making mailing labels available. Rose said he liked the idea but that an updated list of players' addresses would not be compiled until sometime in November.

He also told me that the MLBPA had a policy against releasing the home addresses of players but that, if I brought the stuffed envelopes to MLBPA headquarters, mailing labels would be affixed to them and they could be mailed from there.

Thereafter, Dr. Hoffmann and I prepared a seven-page questionnaire with 61 questions. Some of the inquiries asked for basic biographical data. Others delved more deeply into likes and dislikes, hopes and fears; and how the individual player's happiness was affected by on-field performance, personal and professional relationships, salary, the media, fans, off-season activities, education, religion, and numerous other variables. *Sports Illustrated* approved the questionnaire with minor changes, and I telephoned Rose to ask how much advance notice would be needed prior to mailing. He said that forty-eight hours would be adequate.

On the first Friday in December, I telephoned the MLBPA to advise Rose that the mailing would be ready in three days and was told by a secretary that he was at the winter meetings in Hawaii and would not be in the office until Monday, December 13. I asked her to call Rose to see if we could proceed with the mailing in his absence. One week later (December 10), she called back, said that Rose had given his go-ahead, and asked if I could bring the envelopes to the MLBPA before noon to be labeled because she was leaving early that day. I said I couldn't but would on Monday. She told me that the office would be too busy on Monday but that I could pick the labels up and mail them myself if I promised that I would make no copies and show them to no one. I agreed (and kept that promise). The questionnaire was sent to 894 players (814 in the United States and 80 in foreign countries).

Then we waited. And the questionnaires began flowing back. The respondents ranged from career utility players to future Hall of Famers. We'd hoped for a cross section of the baseball community, and we got it. Some of the names were familiar to me. Others meant nothing until I began reading their answers and then they became flesh and blood.

The overwhelming majority of players said that their happiest moment in baseball was their first major league game. Others mentioned their first major league hit or first major league home run. Playing in the World Series and winning the World Series were also cited by those who'd had that experience. Pitchers frequently referenced their first major league win, although one hurler noted a bases-loaded double against Nolan Ryan as his happiest moment and another wrote, "striking out Reggie Jackson."

On the opposite side of the coin, when players were asked about their most unhappy moment in baseball, the most common answer was "being sent back down to the minors." Others cited the first time they were traded, although most saw trades as part of the game. The consensus was that it was a lot better to be traded to a first-place team than to a lesser club. Other unhappy moments derived from a poor individual performance such as "giving up five home runs in a game" or "striking out four times in one game." Another player's most unhappy moment was "when we were in the World Series and I didn't get into a game."

When asked to identify their greatest professional fear, players overwhelmingly cited the fear of a career-ending injury. "Pitchers never know when their arm is going to blow out," one respondent wrote. "It's just a matter of time."

Were players worried in general about their career coming to an end?

"The worries began on day one," one player answered. "It's a fact of life."

Quite a few voiced regret that they weren't better educated so that their career options would be more varied when their playing days were over. "It's a fantasy world, and you have to prepare for when you are out of it," one player wrote.

Fear of failure in single-game situations wasn't as pronounced as we'd thought it would be. Professionals understand that losing is part of the game. We also hadn't expected the response of a pitcher who told us that his greatest fear was "someone shooting me when I'm on the mound."

One of the questions we asked was, "Do you ever get depressed about your professional career? If so, what causes it?"

Most of the players acknowledged having been depressed at one time or another. Injury was a common cause of depression. Other causes were a lack of playing time, poor performance on the field, and a lack of job security. "I'm trying never-endingly to fill the void whenever I get depressed," one player wrote. None of the respondents said that they got depressed because their team was losing.

Quite a few of the players had considered quitting baseball at one time or another, usually when they were mired in the minor leagues or were sent back down to the minors after a stint in the big leagues. One player (who ultimately had an eleven-year major league career) admitted that he'd been very close to quitting. "Never played much, was shown up by manager," he wrote. "I didn't [quit] because it was just one man's judgment."

The thing that players seemed to dislike most about major league ball was the travel. They found it tiring and anxiety-provoking. "I don't fear flying," one player told us. "But everyone in the back of their mind thinks about crashing."

Questions about fans elicited a range of responses. One question we asked was, "Do you feel that the fans understand and fully appreciate your skills?"

"The true fans understand," one player responded. But other players answered "no" followed by comments such as, "They don't realize how complicated and demanding the job is. The game looks too easy from the stands . . . They don't know what it takes to be a player. They think it's easy because they've seen it been made to look easy by great players."

Another question ("Do you feel that the fans understand and fully appreciate your problems?") evoked a passionate response. At one end of the spectrum were players who answered, "The fans shouldn't have to understand my problems . . . I don't expect them to. I would rather the fans not know my personal problems."

But most players answered "no" followed by thoughts like, "No way . . . All the fans see is the good times . . . They only see the glamour of playing in the big leagues . . . They don't know the everyday pressure of playing . . . They don't realize the pressures involved . . . Very few fans have any idea what a ballplayer goes through . . . Fans don't realize the feeling you have when you go 0-4 that day . . . Most fans don't comprehend what being a professional athlete is all about. They view it with rose colored glasses and envy . . . They make us out to be more than we are. After all, we are just people with the ability to play baseball . . . They think life in the big leagues is all fun and games. They don't realize the hardships and that this is more than a game. It's my job . . . Most fans don't feel the players are human. We're supposed to be at our peak all the time . . . Most people don't realize how hard a 162-game season is. Travel, sickness, family problems. There is not a player in either league that feels 100% for every game. Some days, you only have 80% in you but you give that full 80%, not 70%

... Fans seem to think this life is one of only glitter and gold. How could anyone making a lot of money have any problems? We're normal people. We have normal problems ... There's no way a fan who attends a baseball game can understand what's going on in my life."

Suspicion of the media was a repeating theme. Comments included, "Most media people just want to sell papers or fill air time and don't care about hurting someone ... They understand our problems, but I don't think they sympathize with us because of the money ... Most writers are frustrated jocks, who second guess you and cannot appreciate the dedication or hardships that playing professional athletics involves ... Most don't care unless you are a star ... The media is disappointingly ignorant about sports and they have no desire to improve."

A majority of players voiced a preference for radio or television over print interviews because they couldn't be misquoted. A sampling of responses on that issue included, "On TV or radio, you say what you say, not what some reporter thinks you should say ... On television or radio, what I say can't be turned around. It's easy to 'misquote' in print ... On radio or television, what comes out of my mouth is what I want people to hear. Print never comes out the same ... On radio or TV, if I am misrepresented, it's nobody's fault but my own."

However, one player preferred print interviews, saying, "It gives you time to think." And another answered, "Radio and television can't really get the whole story right in five minutes. But print is only better when the story is printed as the player said it, not the way the writer heard it."

The feeling across the board was that Spanish-speaking players had an extra set of problems because of language barriers. Remember; in 1982, there were far fewer Hispanics in the major leagues than there are today.

Another question we asked was, "Are your reasons for continuing to play ball different now from when you started?" Representative answers included, "When I played in little league and high school, we had a lot of fun. In the pros, it's serious business ... At first, I played to satisfy my dream and to make it to the big leagues. Now I play to support my family and set up my future financially ... I started for fun. Now it's a business ... When I started in the game, it was for fun. The older I got, the fun went away and the business took over ... The fun is slowly being taken out of it. It's a job now."

Clearly, money was a major incentive. But virtually without exception, the respondents said that they'd rather play regularly and make $200,000 than sit on the bench for $300,000. Although one player noted, "If I'm playing regularly, I'll get to $300,000." And another observed, "You can't renegotiate your contract while you're sitting on the bench."

"Do you think you'll be more or less happy than you are now when you're no longer playing?"

"Less happy," one player answered. "I'll always miss not being able to play. Not everyone can make 50,000 people stand up and cheer." But another player answered, "More happy. All the pressures will be over."

And there were numerous nuggets of information.

"How did you feel when Hank Aaron broke Babe Ruth's record?"

"It made me proud to be a part of a profession that produces these types of people."

"Do you like giving autographs?"

"Not to adults. Yes, to little kids. You really make their day."

"What do you like most about playing major league ball?"

"The way little kids look up to you."

Another question we asked was, "If you could change places with any player, who would it be?"

Most players said that they were happy being who they were. But pitchers entertained the fantasy of changing places more often than position players; and the player they most often wanted to change places with was Steve Carlton ("He has been the best pitcher in both leagues for the past ten seasons . . . He has one of the best mental attitudes in the game . . . He does his job as well as anyone and works hard at it . . . He has changed with the game and has an awesome pitch and he can hit too . . . I think he's the best").

Other pitchers on the list included Tom Seaver ("because he has done everything in his career that I hope to accomplish in mine"), Gaylord Perry ("for his consistency and accomplishments"), Phil Neikro ("class and money and fame"), Jim Palmer ("he is my idol"), Storm Davis ("has great attitude and talent and is 20 years old"), and Nolan Ryan ("I just want to make what he pays in taxes each year").

Rod Carew was the only position player with whom multiple respondents said they'd be willing to change places.

Regarding another superstar, one player wrote, "With the wife and kids I have and the close friends who live near, nobody could have it any better than I do. If I did [want to change places], it would be with a player whose career is so fantastic that the players he played with and against would say he was the best ever at that position. Not the media or fans, but the players. They are the ones I would want the respect from. The one man would be Johnny Bench."

Many of the players said that their happiness sprang from a belief in God. Their religious faith was extremely important to them. Another wrote, "The luck factor in baseball and all sports puzzles me."

One comment that I found thought provoking was, "I think every player should have one great great year just to see what it feels like. Both individual and team-wise, very few do."

Significantly, a dominant theme in the responses was a love of the game: "Baseball has been in my life since I was six years old, and I enjoy it as much now as then. I wish I could give baseball as much as it has given me . . . I'm doing what I've wanted to do since I was a little boy . . . I'm doing something that every kid dreams of doing . . . I like the fact that I'm playing at the highest level of competition there is in my profession . . . It's a hard road. But if you make it, it's very rewarding . . . I'm 38 and still in love with the game . . . All I ever wanted was to play baseball. My goal was to make it to the major leagues. Now that I am here, it makes all those sacrifices worth it. I would not change my nine years of pro ball for anything . . . Baseball is a beautiful game that's been changed by modern science and media types and aluminum bats and gloves with flashing lights. It's hard to concentrate on just the game sometimes, but that makes me love it that much more. I hope I never stop playing baseball."

But the most gratifying thing about the responses was the way that many players reacted to the project itself. Some acknowledged having sought help from a psychiatrist or other psychotherapists in the past, and all but one considered it to have been a worthwhile experience.

Beyond that, we got comments such as, "Your questions show thought and much deliberation. It is a good questionnaire . . . This sounds interesting. I would like to see the finished product . . . This is good. People might start realizing that ballplayers have emotions and feelings and aren't just a baseball card . . . Baseball is strenuous, both physically and mentally. If there's anything to take a little of the stress off of us by filling this out, I'm all for it."

The final question on the questionnaire was, "Would you be willing to discuss any of these issues further? If so, how would you like us to contact you?" More than half of the players answered "yes" and wrote in their home address or telephone number.

"If you want the actual truth," one player told us, "several times I was tempted to withhold something because it was insulting or something that could be used against me later. All the issues are open. Please call."

We never got the chance.

The questionnaire had been mailed to players on the second weekend in December. On Friday, December 17, Marvin Miller telephoned me. He was not a happy camper.

Miller told me that he had never been informed of the project and asked for a chronology of what had occurred. I explained the undertaking and recounted the events that led up to the questionnaire being mailed to members of the MLBPA. Miller's comments and tone of voice made it clear that a hard road lay ahead.

'Is there any way we can salvage the project?" I asked.

"That's my decision, not yours," Miller answered.

Then the steady stream of responses stopped. A few more filtered in, but not many. Finally, we received one last questionnaire from a player who wrote on the last page, "I got a letter from the players association regarding your questionnaire. However, I think it is a worthwhile survey so I filled it out anyway. Call me."

The player gave us his home telephone number. He also enclosed a December 21, 1982, memorandum that had been sent to all members of the MLBPA by Marvin Miller.

Miller's memorandum began as follows: "Early this month, two writers, Thomas Hauser and William Hoffmann, sent a letter and a questionnaire to all major league baseball players. The letter stated that the purpose of the questionnaire was to obtain material for a proposed article in *Sports Illustrated*."

Miller went on to state, "The questionnaire, with its 61 questions, was never seen by me or any staff member of the Players Association prior to its being sent to players." Miller's letter further advised recipients that the secretary who had given us the addresses had been fired, and closed with the suggestion, "If you have not yet responded to the questionnaire, you may wish to consider whether you should ignore it in light of what has happened."

Miller's letter was carefully worded. Without directly saying so, he was telling the players to not respond to the survey. I telephoned him. He wouldn't take my call. I wrote him a letter voicing my displeasure. He sent me back an unpleasant response. That was the end of communication between us.

The project was dead. Eighty-four players had returned the questionnaire. That wasn't enough for a valid statistical study. And there was no way our research could proceed to stage two; follow-up interviews with the players who'd indicated a willingness to talk with us.

There was a glimmer of hope in 1983, when Miller was succeeded by Kenneth Moffett as executive director of the Major League Baseball Players Association. Later that year, I telephoned Moffett, explained what had happened, and broached the subject of trying again. Moffett asked me to send him copies of the questionnaire and related correspondence, which I did. Several days later, he telephoned and said, "I'm sorry. I'd love to help you on this. It seems like a worthwhile study, but my hands are tied. I'm in a very difficult position here. Marvin would never allow it."

Two months later, Moffett was dismissed as executive director of the MLBPA. Miller returned to serve as interim executive director until a replacement was named.

And that was that. I put the questionnaires in a closet and went on to other things. Time passed. Bill Hoffmann died of cancer in October 2000. His death was a tragedy and a terrible blow to all who loved him. Recently, on a whim, I decided to look at the questionnaires again. Almost a quarter-century had passed since I'd first seen them.

"Baseball is a great game and it's a great profession if you can keep everything in perspective," read the first questionnaire I looked at. "Ballplayers are normal people, and we encounter many of the same problems most people run into."

Why did Miller do what he did? I think he was angry that the questionnaire had been sent out without his knowledge. Would he have approved the project if it had run through him? I don't know. It might be that the information we were gathering would have made him nervous. After all, Miller served his players brilliantly on economic issues. His legacy failed when it came to illegal drugs, which continue to endanger the health of union members. And he could have done more to make the players better understood and more sympathetic figures in the eyes of fans.

Are baseball players happy (or were they happy in 1982)? The responses we got seemed to indicate that players have more highs and lows than the average person; a greater sense of opportunity, but also a sense of how fragile that opportunity is.

I also know that some of the comments we received from players were particularly well thought out and seemed to come from special people. I'm sorry that we never had an opportunity to get to know them.

This article was written for the Sunday Times (of London) in 2004.

Arnold Palmer at Seventy-Five

Great athletes come and go in sports, but only a few change the way their sport is perceived. Muhammad Ali did it with boxing. Pele did it with soccer. And Arnold Palmer did it with golf. Now a milestone is at hand. On September 10, "Arnie" turns seventy-five.

Palmer has aged well. There are a few chronic aches in his hip and shoulder; the sort of ailments that afflict most people, and particularly golfers, as they age. Last month, he observed, "Getting old is not for sissies." But there has been no reoccurrence of the prostate cancer that Palmer was operated on for in 1997. Overall, his health is good.

Palmer still spends May 1 through October 1 of each year in Latrobe, Pennsylvania, where he was born and raised. He now owns the golf course where he learned the game as a boy. Then, as the autumn leaves turn, he relocates to Orlando, Florida, where he is president and principal owner of the two-hundred-acre Bay Hill Club and Lodge.

Palmer's house in Latrobe and condominium at Bay Hill are modest given his enormous financial holdings. Both homes are tastefully decorated. The most valuable work of art in either of them is a pastoral scene that hangs in the living room in Pennsylvania; a painting given to Palmer at a surprise birthday party in 1966 by the artist, Dwight Eisenhower.

Palmer is also an accomplished pilot. He took his first flying lessons in 1956 and began soloing two years later. He now owns a Cessna Citation X; the top-of-the-line Citation jet, capable of flying at 600 miles an hour. In June 2004, he flew himself non-stop from Latrobe to Scotland for the 250th anniversary celebration of the Royal and Ancient Golf Club of St. Andrews.

And of course, Palmer is still playing golf. Earlier this year, he played in his fiftieth Masters at Augusta. He now says that was his last event on the regular PGA tour. But he's on the course almost every day and plans to enter five or six tournaments next year on the Champions (Seniors) Tour.

"I still enjoy playing," he says. "It's not as much fun as it once was because I don't play as well as I used to and that takes a toll after a while. I play with people I know I should beat, and then I don't play well enough to win. But I look forward to every day; I'm still working on my game; and I'm still trying to find a way to hit the ball further."

How does Palmer feel about turning seventy-five?

"It's too damn old," he answers.

What does he envision happening in the future?

"I don't think I'll ever retire. I'll just fade away."

It's hard to imagine Arnold Palmer going quietly. The son of a construction worker who later became a greens keeper and then a club pro, Palmer was responsible for a whole new audience becoming interested in golf. There was a time when his losing a golf tournament was more interesting than almost anyone else winning. He stirred passions and created a sense of sharing his adventures on the course in a way that no other golfer ever has.

Palmer seemed to have been made in the image of every mother's loving son and every man's best friend. He was the boy next door; confident and reassuring but never arrogant. Men thought of him as a man's man. Women found him charming, handsome, magnetic, and strong. He was bold, charismatic, a bit impatient, a winner who succeeded at everything he did and still seemed like a regular guy.

Palmer was "everyman" in an elitist sport. His style of play was, "Hit it hard; go find it; and hit it hard again." His ability to perform under pressure, and the frequency with which he came from behind mirrored and reinforced the image of his personality. He didn't just play a course; he attacked each hole as though intent on obliterating par. Spectators couldn't turn away for an instant because at any moment—BOOM—something might happen.

Arnie's Army (as his fans became known) expected Arnold to find trouble on the golf course; and then they expected him to play the role of cavalry soldier riding over the hill to save himself from disaster. He viewed lakes, streams, sand bunkers, and trees as minor nuisances, not hazards. And he was a warrior, who plied his trade with intensity and determination. Palmer on the golf course radiated decency and grace, but also an all-consuming desire to win. "I'd rather win one tournament in my life than make the cut every week." he said.

Palmer won the United States Golf Association Amateur Championship in 1954 and turned pro later that year. He captured his first Masters championship in 1958, but his greatest glories lay ahead.

No year ever meant more to a sport than 1960 meant to golf, and the man with the magic wand was Palmer. He won his second Masters at Augusta in April and arrived at the U.S. Open with five tournament victories for the season. When the Open was done, the Palmer Legend was on the rise to near-mythic proportions.

From 1898 through 1965, the last two rounds of the U.S. Open were played on the same day. Palmer began "Open Saturday" in 1960 with a morning-round 72 that left him in fifteenth place, seven strokes off the lead and well behind established pros like Ben Hogan and Sam Snead. He then proceeded to birdie six of the first seven final-round holes en route to a closing 65. That made him only the third man in history to win the Masters and U.S. Open in the same year. At the time, it was the lowest final-round score ever for a U.S. Open champion.

By the summer of 1960, Palmer's popularity in the United States was so great that newspapers and magazines were giving extra coverage to golf. Reporters were told to place his name high in stories, regardless of how he fared in a tournament. By year's end, he had emerged victorious in eight tournaments, finished in the top five in 19 out of 29 tournaments entered, and become the most popular athlete in America. *Sports Illustrated* named him "Sportsman of the Year." A poll of sportswriters awarded him the prestigious Hickock Belt as "Professional Athlete of the Year." He was the young Tiger Woods. Or to be more accurate, the young Tiger Woods was a reincarnation of Arnold Palmer in his prime.

In 1961, Palmer added a British Open championship to his resume. 1962 began with more of the same, including a third Masters triumph. By that time, to quote sportswriter Dan Jenkins, Palmer had become "something of a worldwide sporting Beatle." Then Jack Nicklaus arrived on the scene.

Nicklaus was ten years younger than Palmer. He wasn't warm or charismatic back then; just an awesomely talented overweight twenty-two-year-old with a butch haircut and high squeaky voice who felt that he was the best golfer in the world and that it was just a matter of time until he proved it.

Palmer's fans "knew" he would win the U.S. Open that year. The tournament would be contested thirty-five miles from Latrobe at the Oakmont Country Club; a course Palmer had played a hundred times. And Arnold played the way everyone thought he would. He shot a four-round 283. To put that number in perspective, in three previous U.S. Opens at Oakmont, only Ben Hogan and Sam Snead had been able to break 290.

But Nicklaus outdid Palmer in the final round of regulation play, closing with a 69 to tie for first place. That set up an eighteen-hole playoff, and Nicklaus carded a 71 to prevail by three strokes. Palmer played magnificent golf. But in many respects that made his defeat even more disheartening because he now knew that, even if he played his best, Nicklaus might beat him. Nicklaus could outdrive him; Nicklaus could putt with him; and Nicklaus just might be the better golfer.

One month after losing to Nicklaus at Oakmont, Palmer won his second "major" of the year with an awesome showing in the British Open. His four-round total of 276 was twelve under par, six strokes ahead of the field, and two strokes better than the previous British Open record. The victory was his seventh "major" championship—a feat made even more impressive by the fact that he was only thirty-two years old; two years younger than Hogan had been when he won the first of his nine major titles. Then, in 1964, Palmer won the Masters for an unprecedented fourth time.

All told, Palmer had 60 victories on the U.S. tour, placing him fourth on the all-time list behind Snead, Nicklaus, and Hogan. His eight "major" titles (including the 1954 USGA Amateur championship) are surpassed by only six other golfers. From 1957 through 1971, he was among the top-ten money winners on the PGA tour. He won at least one PGA tournament every year from 1955 through 1971; a remarkable seventeen-season run. On four occasions, he captured the Vardon Trophy, awarded annually to the golfer with the lowest official-tournament scoring average. In one five-year span, from 1960 through 1964, he entered nineteen "majors" and won six while finishing in the top-five fourteen times and in the top-ten on sixteen occasions.

But more important than individual victories was the impact that Palmer had on the world of golf. No less a personage than Jack Nicklaus has declared, "Arnold's place in history will be as the man who took golf from being a game for the few to a sport of the masses. He was the catalyst who made that happen."

Palmer was also the catalyst for a revolution in the economics of sports. He was the first athlete to parlay success on the playing field into lucrative endorsement contracts. With the aid of Mark McCormack (who later founded IMG), he virtually invented the role of the athlete-entrepreneur and created a massive corporate empire.

Before Palmer and McCormack joined forces, no one had understood the extent to which major sports personalities could be linked to profitable business ventures. But McCormack had a theory—that people love athletes; and where Palmer in particular was concerned, they trusted "Arnie" and wanted to help him. Thus, McCormack approached corporations with the suggestion that they license Palmer's name as a way of identifying their products with the Palmer standard of excellence.

"Arnold Palmer is a brand name," McCormack told them. "When you license the Palmer name, you're buying an image of quality, goodness, honesty, and sincerity. And a licensing agreement with Arnold will cost you far less than it would cost to build a brand name from scratch."

It's not just golfers who are indebted to Palmer today. Every athlete with multimillion-dollar endorsement income can trace the roots of his or her financial success to Palmer. And the most extraordinary aspect of his commercial appeal has been its longevity. For thirty consecutive years, he was the top-grossing athlete in the world in terms of endorsement income. Finally, in 1991, Michael Jordan surpassed him.

Palmer still loves golf. And the world of golf still loves him, even though his last victory on the PGA Tour was in 1973 and he last played in the U.S. Open and PGA championships in 1994.

"We've all watched that scene at the Masters or U.S. Open where the leader comes down the fairway to the final green with the crowd cheering," sportscaster Dick Schaap reminisced a decade ago. "And with Arnold Palmer, that scene was as exhilarating and thrilling as anything in sports."

Certainly, British fans appreciate the Palmer magic. A half-century ago, the British Open was a "major" championship by tradition, but one that had fallen on hard times. Most of the world's best players avoided the event, because to enter they were required to play in a thirty-six-hole qualifying tournament. And even if they were successful, the prize money was minimal.

"I played the British Open," Byron Nelson recalled. "It took a week to get there and a week to get home. I was the low American; finished fourth or fifth. And what it came down to was, I lost a good part of my summer, won $185, and spent a thousand dollars on boat fare alone."

But Palmer passionately wanted his name on the Claret Jug. "And by going to St. Andrews," Gary Player later said, "Arnold almost singlehandedly returned the British Open to its rightful position of grandeur."

Henry Longhurst agreed and wrote of Palmer's first British Open triumph, "It is doubtful that there was a man present at Birkdale who wanted Palmer to lose. It's impossible to overpraise the tact and charm with which this American has conducted himself on his two visits to Britain. He has no fancy airs or graces; he wears no fancy clothes; he makes no fancy speeches. He simply says and does exactly the right thing at the right time, and that is enough."

There are two memories of the British Open that stand out in Palmer's mind. On the sixteenth hole of the final round in 1961, his third shot landed right of the green in a bush. "The longer I studied it, the worse it looked," he later said. "But then I walked up on the green, and the first thing that struck me was I could see the ball. That meant there had to be an avenue for escape, so I took my sand wedge and laid it wide open." The ball rose high in the air and came to rest two feet from the cup. The subsequent putt gave Palmer a par 5. He won the tournament by a single stroke.

And then there's the memory of walking down the fairway toward the final hole of what Palmer knew would be his last British Open in 1995. "It was a bittersweet moment," he remembers. "The gallery was wonderful; people couldn't have been nicer. It was satisfying to know that the good things happened and how people felt about them. But it was sad to know that those things wouldn't be happening for me anymore."

Four years later, there was greater sadness. On November 20, 1999, Arnold's wife of forty-five years—Winifred Walzer Palmer—died of cancer at age sixty-five. "Winnie" tried to stay out of the limelight, but she had always been there for Arnold when he needed her. She'd been the mainstay in raising two daughters, kept the house, and done all the cooking herself. Early in Arnold's career, she'd handled most of his business arrangements. Throughout their life together, she was his most trusted advisor.

Arnold's legacy with Winnie includes two daughters and seven grandchildren. Meanwhile, Palmer is now engaged to Kathleen "Kit" Gawthrop; a longtime family friend in her late-sixties, who lives just outside of San Francisco. They've been dating for about a year and plan to marry in 2005. "I have a new kind of life now," he says. "And Kit is very important to me. She's helping to make my life a happier life."

Following my celebration of Arnold Palmer's seventy-fifth birthday, I added a political-personal note.

The Political Side of Arnold Palmer

As the United States readies for the 2004 presidential election, political memories come to mind. I've spent a lot of time with Muhammad Ali, who embodied one set of values in the turbulent 1960s. But I'm also familiar with sportsmen who championed the opposite side of the political equation.

In 1992, I was approached by representatives of Arnold Palmer, who asked if I'd be interested in writing a book about Palmer's life. The invitation came on the heels of my having authored *Muhammad Ali: His Life And Times*. Following the success of that project, I'd been offered (and declined) numerous "celebrity" books. But the thought of working with, and learning more about, Palmer appealed to me. His impact on golf, his role in redefining the economics of sports, and his influence as an American icon have been enormous.

In December 1992, I journeyed to Orlando, Florida, where Palmer keeps his winter home. Each morning, Arnold and I would sit in his office; I'd turn on my tape recorder; and we'd talk. Then Arnold would have a bowl of soup and go out to play eighteen holes of golf. I'm not a golfer, but I'd walk the course with him.

One of the things that Palmer and I discussed in our morning sessions was politics.

"My father was a Democrat," Arnold told me. "He thought Franklin Roosevelt hung the moon, but I'm the opposite. I think you solve problems through family and personal charity. The less that big government and big-name outsiders get involved, the better it is for us all."

"I have strong opinions," Palmer elaborated. "But I've made a conscious decision not to make a big issue of them publicly. I voice my opinions to my friends and family, generally in a conservative way. There are times when I'm tempted to be more outspoken; but usually I think about it for a day or two and pull in because I don't want to be like a lot of people who I hear voicing opinions publicly. So when I'm outraged about something, politically or whatever, I express myself in the office and at home. Then I hear from the people who've heard me; and it's rare that I get a hundred percent agreement on what I've said, so I drop it."

Given the appeal of Palmer's personality and the strength of his views, the possibility of his becoming a candidate for public office was discussed many times. Indeed, he had been asked by Republican Party leaders to run for governor in his home state of Pennsylvania on a half-dozen occasions.

"I don't think Arnie ever seriously entertained the idea of running for governor," his wife, Winnie, told me. "At least, I hope not. He was flattered by it. But I was very much against it, and always will be. Knowing Arnie as well as I do, I think being in politics would eat him up. I just don't think Arnie is made for politics."

It's easy to imagine a Palmer campaign patterned on those of Ronald Reagan. The public has always seen what it wants to see in Arnold. He's a conservative multi-millionaire tycoon who has supported eleven Republican candidates for president in a row. Yet, in the steel mills and coal mines of middle America, he remains a working-class hero. That's a pretty good political base.

When I started working with Arnold, playing golf with him had become almost mandatory for presidents of the United States. Thus, one of the questions I asked was how he would assess the golf games of the various presidents he'd played with.

"General Eisenhower was certainly a better player than the average American who played golf," Palmer told me. "He hit the ball pretty well, but the strongest part of his game was his desire. He had other hobbies, but I don't think any of them meant as much to him as golf. Richard Nixon wasn't really a golfer. Gerald Ford had an eighteen handicap and deserved every bit of it, but he hit the ball hard and at times played very well. Ford's problem was, he had the yips putting. George Bush [the elder Bush] plays to a fourteen handicap and, now that he has more free time, I think his game will get better."

Later that day, after Palmer finished his bowl of soup, he went out to play golf. I walked with him. Arnold was playing brilliantly. Through twelve holes, he was four strokes under par on the course where the Bay

Hill Invitational (an official PGA Tour event) is played each year. And remember; at the time, he was sixty-three years old.

Arnold's drive off the thirteenth tee split the fairway. As he walked the two hundred yards toward his ball, I asked what I thought was an innocent question about the man who, one month earlier, had been elected president of the United States: "Apropos of what we were talking about this morning, would you like to play golf with Bill Clinton?"

Six months later, Clinton and Palmer would, in fact, play together. And Arnold would tell me, "Bill Clinton has the potential to be a very good golfer. He putts the ball very well. He's strong and has a keen interest in the game. His swing is pretty good and he has a lot of determination to be a good player."

But that was in the future. On this particular day, Arnold answered, "I suppose so. I'd be interested in seeing what kind of game he plays and what he's like as a person. Of course, if you want my opinion, I don't think Bill Clinton cares one bit about the average person. I think Bill Clinton is nothing but a phony. Bill Clinton . . ."

Arnold was getting madder and madder.

Then he hit his next shot into the pond that fronted the thirteenth green.

"Uh oh," I told myself. "I've got a big problem."

Arnold turned to me with a look that was more glare than smile. "Why did I lose my concentration like that?" he asked rhetorically.

Then he took a penalty drop and wound up with a double-bogey six. He later rallied to finish the round with a four-under-par sixty-eight.

He didn't mention Bill Clinton again that day. And for obvious reasons, neither did I.

As decades pass, college basketball moves ever more distant from its roots. The thoughts below were penned in 2004.

Invite Everyone to the Dance

You see it on television every year on the day that has become known as "Selection Sunday." Young men who play basketball for teams "on the bubble" anxiously sit and wait. Then the NCAA men's championship basketball tournament brackets are announced, bringing joy to some and tears to others.

The first NCAA men's basketball championship final was played in 1939 at the Patten Gym in Evanston, Illinois, in front of 5,500 fans. Total attendance for the tournament was 15,025. The tournament ran a deficit of $2,531.

1954 was the first year in which the NCAA basketball championship game was televised nationally. Event organizers were paid a television license fee of $7,500. The first reference to "final four" in an NCAA publication came in 1975. The term wasn't even capitalized until it appeared in the *1978 NCAA Official Collegiate Basketball Guide.*

By contrast, over the past eight years, no NCAA men's basketball championship final has been played before fewer than 40,000 fans. Total attendance for the tournament exceeds 700,000 annually. CBS now pays a license fee of $350 million a year to televise the tournament.

In sum, the NCAA tournament has become big business. The NCAA has trademarked the term "March Madness." "Sweet Sixteen" and "Elite Eight" now qualify as hoops terminology. But along the way, the professed ideal of college sports—participation in a shared learning experience—has been lost.

Here's a proposal to remedy the situation. On college campuses, the homecoming dance is open to all students; not just the dozen-or-so who have a realistic chance of being voted homecoming king and queen. Likewise, there are 327 teams that play NCAA Division I basketball. Let's invite every one of them to the dance. And what's good for the men would be good for the women too.

There's nothing sacrosanct about 65 teams being invited to the NCAA tournament. That's the current number (63 teams plus two that participate in a play-in game). But from 1939 through 1950, only eight teams were invited. The following two years, the number was 16. From 1953 through 1974, the number fluctuated between 20 and 25. Since then, the total has climbed steadily upward: 1975–1978 (32 teams); 1979 (40 teams); 1980–1982 (48 teams); 1983 (52 teams); 1984 (53 teams); 1985–2000 (64 teams); and 2001 to date (65 teams).

How would the new system work? Start with the 142 teams that are ranked #186 through #327 facing off against one another. The 71 winners of those games would join the teams ranked #1 through #185 to form a field of 256. Two more rounds would narrow the tournament to the present 64.

In other words, you're adding three rounds to the tournament. And before anyone gets too excited about student athletes missing all that classroom time, consider the fact that inviting everyone to the dance would be an ideal reason to kill the banal post-season conference tournaments, which require three or more extra games for the winners and are little more than an exercise to determine who goes to the dance and how they're seeded.

Also, keep in mind that it's highly unlikely that any of the first-round teams would make it through six games (which is what the two NCAA finalists currently play each year), let alone nine.

It's time to share the experience of March Madness. 2004 will be the twentieth year in a row that Arizona has appeared in the tournament. Kentucky has been to the dance forty-five times. But many schools have never gone.

Obviously, a team that's ranked in the bottom two hundred isn't going to win the tournament. In all likelihood, none of those teams would last past the early rounds. But make no mistake about it. There would be upsets. Since the tournament went to 64 teams in 1985, a #16 seed has never beaten a #1. But #15 has beaten #2 four times. And for many teams, even a first-round victory would become an important part of school lore.

One of the joys of the New York City Marathon is that the race is open to everyone. 99.9 percent of the runners who enter understand that they have no chance of winning. But they want to be part of a great athletic competition. They want to be able to say that they ran in the same race as the greatest runners in the world. The NCAA should offer no less to the student athletes who play basketball at its Division I schools.

In 2005, the Observer Sports Monthly asked me to compile a list of the ten greatest moments in American sports, ranking them from #1 through #10. When the article was published, I was mortified to see that the rankings had been reordered. The explanation given to me was, "This way, they fit better with the photographs." My original list follows.

The Ten Greatest Moments in American Sports

Professional sports is deeply ingrained in the fabric of America. It's an economic force, a spawning ground for heroes, and for many, a way of life.

Over the years, certain sports landmarks have achieved near-mythical status in the United States. Here's one person's list of the ten greatest moments in American sports.

(1) Joe Louis Defeats Max Schmeling (1938)

The Great Depression was ravaging America. War clouds had gathered in Europe. And Joe Louis was heavyweight champion of the world. All of Louis's fights encompassed the issue of race, but Louis-Schmeling II went beyond that. The bout spoke to issues of democracy and totalitarianism. It was viewed as a test of decency and freedom versus Nazi philosophy. For the first time ever, many white Americans openly rooted for a black man against a white opponent.

Schmeling had KO'd the Brown Bomber in 1936. After Louis defeated James Braddock for the heavyweight crown, Louis-Schmeling II became inevitable. Their rematch was heard live on radio throughout the world. It lasted 124 seconds. On that night, twenty-four-year-old Joe Louis was the greatest fighter who ever lived.

(2) The Baltimore Colts Beat the New York Giants to Win the
National Football League Championship (1958)

Football is the most popular sport in the United States. Its rise began
when the Baltimore Colts beat the New York Giants 23–17 in what his-
torians call "the greatest football game ever played."

The Colts jumped to a 14–3 advantage, but the Giants came back
with two late touchdowns for a 17–14 lead. With seven seconds left on
the clock, Steve Myhra of Baltimore kicked a twenty-yard field goal to tie
the score. Time expired. For the first time ever, an NFL championship
game would be decided in sudden-death overtime.

Baltimore was led by Johnny Unitas, the premier quarterback in NFL
history. In the extra stanza, he drove his team inexorably down the field.
Eight minutes, fifteen seconds into overtime, Alan Ameche dove into the
end zone for a touchdown. Baltimore had prevailed.

(3) The Boston Red Sox Rally to Beat the New York Yankees (2004)

Since 1923, the New York Yankees have won the World Series
twenty-six times. By contrast, the Boston Red Sox were long considered
"lovable losers." They hadn't won a World Series since 1918. In 1986,
Boston was one out away from victory when the dream ended with a
wild pitch followed by a ground ball that dribbled through their first baseman's legs.

2004 seemed like more of the same. The Red Sox advanced to the
second round of the playoffs; then fell behind the hated Yankees three
games to none. But the "impossible" happened. Incredibly, Boston swept
the next four games, advanced to the World Series, and defeated the St.
Louis Cardinals in four straight games to capture its first championship in
eighty-six years.

(4) Arnold Palmer Wins the U.S. Open (1960)

After three rounds of the 1960 U.S. Open, Arnold Palmer was in fifteenth place, seven strokes off the lead. So he went out and birdied six of
the first seven holes en route to a final-round 65. That gave him a narrow
victory over Ben Hogan and a twenty-year-old amateur named Jack

Nicklaus. But more impressive than the fact that Palmer had won was the manner in which he'd come from behind with what was fast becoming his trademark charge. "Arnie's Army" was born; the links had their first telegenic superstar; and golf was on its way to becoming a "major" sport in America.

(5) Secretariat Wins the Belmont Stakes to Capture the Triple Crown (1973)

Thoroughbred racing needed an attraction to rejuvenate the sport. Then Secretariat came along. The chestnut colt won the Kentucky Derby and Preakness by 2 1/2 lengths each. If jockey Ron Turcotte could guide his horse to victory in the Belmont Stakes, Secretariat would become racing's first "triple crown" winner in twenty-five years.

At Belmont, Turcotte was just along for the ride. Secretariat put on the greatest performance in racing history, shattering Gallant Man's track record by 2 3/5 seconds, the equivalent of thirteen lengths. The closest competitor finished thirty-one lengths back. In the stretch run, no other horse appeared on the television monitor.

(6) Joe Frazier beats Muhammad Ali (1971)

The 1960s had exploded. America was torn apart by assassinations, urban riots, Vietnam, and counterculture rebellion. In sports, two men were symbolic of the divide. "What you had that night," television commentator Bryant Gumbel later recalled, "were two undefeated heavyweight champions. One was the very symbol of black pride, parading black feelings about black heritage, speaking out against racial injustice. And the other guy just kind of went along. After a while, how you stood on Ali became a political and generational litmus test."

It was the most anticipated, most heavily promoted event in the history of sports. Frazier won over fifteen brutal rounds.

(7) The United States Hockey Team Upsets the Soviet Union at Lake Placid (1980)

The Soviet Union had invaded Afghanistan. Americans were being held hostage in Iran. The country needed a boost. But no one thought that the U.S. Olympic hockey team would provide it. The USSR had won four consecutive Olympic gold medals. The U.S. was seeded seventh in an eight-team draw. Three days before the Olympics began, the Americans were routed by the Soviets in an exhibition game 10 to 3.

At Lake Placid, the U.S. tied Sweden and won its next four outings. Then came the Olympic semifinals. The Soviets led 2–1 in the waning moments of the first period. With one second left on the clock, the U.S. knotted the score. The Soviets regained the lead in the second stanza and held it until 8:39 of the third period. Then, in the span of 81 seconds, the U.S. scored two goals. Final score: U.S. 4, USSR 3. Two days later, the Americans beat Finland 4–2 to capture the gold medal.

(8) The Boston Celtics Beat the Los Angeles Lakers in Bill Russell's Final Game (1969)

From 1957 through 1969, the Boston Celtics were the greatest dynasty in the history of sports, winning eleven National Basketball Association championships in thirteen years. The cornerstone of that dynasty was Bill Russell.

On the court, Russell and Wilt Chamberlain engaged in one of sports' greatest rivalries. Chamberlain led the league in scoring seven years in a row and in rebounding eleven times. Russell copped four rebounding titles and won five Most Valuable Player awards to Wilt's four. Their final confrontation came in the seventh and deciding game of the 1969 NBA championships. Boston eked out a 108–106 win. After the victory, Russell retired.

(9) Mark Spitz Wins Seven Gold Medals at the Munich Olympics (1972)

The 1972 Olympics are remembered for the murder of eleven Israeli athletes by Palestinian terrorists. But they were also the games at which Mark Spitz won an astonishing seven gold medals.

Spitz had earned individual silver and bronze medals plus two golds in relay events as an eighteen-year-old in 1968. In Munich, he won gold in the 100- and 200-meter freestyle and 100- and 200-meter butterfly coupled with three relay triumphs. Each of his 1972 victories came in world-record time.

(10) Jackie Robinson Breaks Baseball's Color Barrier (1947)

Beginning in the late nineteenth century, black players had been barred from playing in baseball's major leagues. On April 15, 1947, with the support of team president Branch Rickey, Jackie Robinson took the field for the Brooklyn Dodgers, scored the winning run, and irrevocably changed sports in America.

Robinson was part of many historic moments. The Dodgers won the pennant that season, and he was named "Rookie of the Year." Two years later, they won it again and he was voted the National League's "Most Valuable Player." Robinson left the game in 1956 and died in 1972.

Robinson's saga might be the most important journey in American sports. To honor his memory, his uniform number, 42, has been retired by every team in Major League Baseball.

I'm not a dog-lover. But some things are hard to resist.

The Westminster Kennel Club Dog Show

Dogs have been part of western culture for as long as . . . Well, for as long as there has been western culture. When Odysseus returned home disguised as a beggar after years of wandering, only his faithful hunting dog recognized him. In Greek mythology, the three-headed Cerberus stood guard at the entrance to Hades.

Millions of Americans grew up watching *Lassie* and *Rin Tin Tin* on television. Depending on their generation, children read *The Call of the Wild* or *The Poky Little Puppy*. The recording industry gave birth to *How Much Is That Doggie in the Window* and *Hound Dog*. Walt Disney bequeathed to us *Lady and the Tramp* and *101 Dalmatians*. The ultimate anthropomorphic dog, of course, is Snoopy of *Peanuts* fame.

Given America's love affair with dogs, it was inevitable that politicians would get into the act. Franklin Roosevelt invoked his dog to mock Republican opponents during the 1944 presidential campaign. It had been charged that FDR sent a naval destroyer to the Aleutian Islands to fetch his terrier that had been left behind after a presidential visit. The story was unfounded, and Roosevelt had a field day with it.

"These Republican leaders have not been content with attacks on me or my wife or my sons," Roosevelt declared. "No; not content with that, now they include my little dog, Fala. I don't resent attacks, but Fala does resent them. He has not been the same dog since."

At the other end of the political spectrum, Richard Nixon relied on a cocker spaniel for political salvation when Dwight Eisenhower considered dumping him from the Republican national ticket in 1952 because of allegations related to a secret "slush fund." Appearing on national television, Nixon acknowledged the fund's existence and then turned his attention to a gift from another supporter.

"It was a little cocker spaniel dog," Nixon told his audience. "Black and white, spotted. Our little girl Tricia, the six-year-old, named it Checkers.

The kids love the dog. And I just want to say this right now; that regardless of what [my political opponents] say about it, we're gonna keep it."

That brings us to the Westminster Kennel Club Dog Show, which was contested earlier this week at Madison Square Garden.

The Westminster Kennel Club was formed by a group of gentlemen who met regularly in New York and decided in 1876 to present a dog show. Adopting the name of the Westminster Hotel in which they met, they held their first show the following year at Gilmore's Gardens on Madison Avenue at 26th Street. Except for a few early shows, the competition has taken place at Madison Square Garden ever since.

Westminster is one of four events to have been held in all four incarnations of Madison Square Garden. The other three are the circus, the National Horse Show, and professional boxing. With the exception of the Kentucky Derby, it's also the oldest continuous sporting event in America. Putting the matter in perspective, when Westminster began, Rutherford B. Hayes was president of the United States; there were thirty-eight states in the Union; and the electric light bulb had not yet been invented.

Westminster is also the most prestigious dog show in the world and gives out five hundred media credentials each year. USA Network televises six hours of the competition, attracting 4.6 million viewers per night, which makes it the network's highest-rated telecast annually.

Over the decades, approximately 270,000 dogs have been entered in Westminster. Contestants are divided into 162 "breeds," which in turn are classified in one of seven "groups." Awards are given for "Best of Breed" (162 awards), "Best in Group" (seven honors), and the ultimate prize: "Best in Show."

Dogs are judged according to American Kennel Club standards. To win any honor, a dog must possess qualities that most closely match the highest standards for its particular breed.

The 2003 Best in Show honor went to a Kerry blue terrier named Torums Scarf Michael. The official standards for Kerry blue terriers decree maximum and minimum heights. They also state, "The correct color is any shade of blue-gray or gray-blue, of a fairly uniform color throughout except that distinctly darker to black parts may appear on the muzzle, head, ears, tail, and feet. Solid black is never permissible in the show ring. Black on the muzzle, head, ears, tail, and feet is permissible. Solid black shall result in disqualification."

That's tough but objective. However, one then comes to the subjective part: "The typical Kerry Blue Terrier should be upstanding, well-knit, and in good balance, showing a well-developed and muscular body with definite terrier style and character throughout . . . The head is long, but not exaggerated, and in good proportion to the rest of the body . . . The hindquarters are strong and muscular with full freedom of action, free from droop or crouch . . . The eyes are dark, small, not prominent, well-placed, and with a keen terrier expression."

And here's the rub. There's only one judge for each category within the competition. In other words, one judge, and one judge alone, chooses Best in Show. The seven group winners are similarly selected. And the 162 Best of Breed honorees are chosen by 162 omnipotent judges.

Thus, one dog owner who has won her share of prizes acknowledges, "If you have nine ordinary dogs and one great one within a breed, the great one will win every time. But if they're relatively equal, three different judges could rule three different ways." And another owner declares, "Let's be honest about it. This is four-legged figure-skating. The dog that has a well-known trainer or a socially-connected owner or a pretty blonde at the other end of the lead has an edge."

Categorized by group, terriers have been Westminster's most consistent winner with forty-three Best in Show honors. By contrast, the herding group has captured Best in Show only once. Top honors have been won by the sporting group fifteen times, the working group on fourteen occasions, nine times each by nonsporting and toy entrants, and three times by hounds.

Not everyone is enamored of Westminster. Jerry Izenberg (the patron saint of sportswriters) was once asked to leave Madison Square Garden while the event was in progress because of an attitude that was deemed unbecoming by show organizers.

"There was a time when dogs guarded castles and pulled wagons through the snow," says Izenberg. "If a St. Bernard is truly the best in its breed, it should be able to climb a mountain in the Swiss Alps with a casket around its neck; but all these dogs do is stand there. I want to see what happens when someone shouts, 'Get help, Muffy!' Will Muffy run through the streets of Manhattan, find a New York City cop, bark, tug at the cuff of the cop's trousers, and, if necessary, subdue the wrongdoers herself? I doubt it."

But Westminster is still special. And heading the list of reasons why is its status as one of the few remaining "benched" shows in the United States. This means that all dogs must arrive in the rotunda adjacent to the main arena by 11:30 AM on the day that their breed is judged and remain there except when being shown in competition until 8:00 PM. During that time, ticketholders are allowed to mingle with the dogs' owners, handlers, and trainers, and even (with permission) pat the dogs.

One gets the impression that Westminster is an elite venture, given the tuxedoed elegance of the ring area and the fact that its Dog Show Committee is studded with names like Thomas H. Bradley III, Frederick W. Wagner III, C. MacNeil Curry III, and Peter R. Van Brunt. But the benching area is marvelously egalitarian; much like a huge indoor flea market with row upon row of dogs ordered by breed.

Walking through the Garden rotunda, the diversity in ownership is clear. At one end of the spectrum are owners who play virtually no role in training or handling their dogs and transport them to shows in Lear jets. At the other end are owners who live in mobile homes and keep their dogs as house pets. Their one common denominator is that the owners are passionate about their dogs. Many of them, including married couples, acknowledge, "Our dogs are our children."

Some owners enter their dogs in shows because they love the scene, the competition, and the prestige of winning. "Have you ever talked to someone who owns a Harley-Davidson?" queries one owner. "You can't explain it. It's in the gut."

An equally common motivation for participation is a desire to improve a given breed. A refrain often heard from owners is, "I love this breed so much, I want to see it made even better."

In other words, Westminster is about the perfectibility of breeds and identifying the best of the best for breeding purposes."

One thing Westminster is not about is making money. Owning a show dog is a good way to go into the red. One doesn't take an adult dog and turn it into a show animal. A dog has to be raised that way.

It starts with a puppy. That's a minimum of a thousand dollars. Then there are trainer fees, handler fees, veterinarian bills, transportation costs to as many as fifty shows a year, and food (these dogs don't eat Alpo). Owners are encouraged to take out paid advertisements featuring their dogs in certain publications; and they do in the belief that it will make their dogs more visible within the small world of dog show judges. It often costs in excess of $50,000 a year to campaign a dog. And virtually no revenue comes in. A dog that wins "Best in Group" at Westminster might command a stud fee of $5,000. But for most dogs, the stud fee is first or second choice of litter. And the only prize for winning Westminster is a trophy.

In contrast to the benching area, the competition itself is a study in glamour. Dogs that are entered receive more grooming than Julia Roberts on the night of the Academy Awards. There are shampoos, conditioners, brushes, combs, stripping knives, scissors, clippers, and (as Yul Brynner once sang) "etcetera, etcetera, and so forth."

Some of the more candid owners acknowledge that a bit of cheating goes on. "There are so many things you can do that are against the rules, but some people do them anyway," admits one owner. Hence the presence of color sticks to make imperfections disappear; white powder for that snowy look; and hairspray on poodles (as opposed to anti-static spray, which is allowed).

Any dog will show better on some days than others. By mid-evening on February 10, 2004, only the seven "Best in Group" winners remained in the competition from the 2,624 dogs that had been entered at Westminster.

The finalists were:

(1) Working group; a Newfoundland named Darbydale's All Rise Pouchcove

(2) Terrier group; a Norfolk Terrier named Cracknor Cause Celebre

(3) Toy group; a Pekingese named Yakee Leaving Me Breathless-AtFranshaw

(4) Non-Sporting group; a standard Poodle named Ale Kai Mikimoto On Fifth

(5) Sporting group; a Sussex Spaniel named Clessexx Three D Grinchy Glee

(6) Hound group; an Ibizan Hound named Luxor's Playmate of the Year

(7) Herding group; a Pembroke Welsh Corgi named Hum'nbird Keepn Up'pearances

Finally, at evening's end, one dog stood alone in the center of Madison Square Garden; Best in Show at Westminster. The winner was Darbydale's All Rise Pouchcove; a huge (155 pounds), lumbering but huggable, black Newfoundland.

All hail the new king.

I don't like mixed martial arts. But it's a phenomenon the boxing world can't ignore. The following article was written in 1997, just as the sport was taking hold in the public consciousness.

Extreme-Ultimate-No-Holds-Barred Fighting

Mixed martial arts competitions aren't very popular in the boxing community these days.

Chris Thorne (president of the Boxing Writers Association of America): "I despise them. They're brutal; they're senseless. It's not a sport; just a another cynical money-making proposition."

Jerry Izenberg (columnist for the *Newark Star-Ledger*): "In order to be an extreme fighting champion, you need every skill that's outlawed on the planet. The very things we pride ourselves on not doing, these people elevate to an art form. I wouldn't even try to dignify it."

Arthur Mercante (boxing's best-known referee): "This type of fighting is particularly damaging to young people because it creates an attitude of rowdyism and incites them with ideas of 'kill.' I think it should be banned."

John Cirillo (president of Madison Square Garden Boxing): "I always start by saying, never say never. But I'd hate to see extreme fighting at Madison Square Garden. I think they go too far."

But then there's Don Elbaum, a boxing guy to the core, who opines "I think extreme fighting is fantastic. I'm dying to see it in person. As long as it doesn't injure anyone else and this is what the fighters want to do, I'm for it all the way."

Mixed martial arts competition goes by many names. But for convenience sake, we'll refer to it here as "extreme fighting." It's generally referred to by the media as "no rules fighting," although there are rules—albeit rules that are still evolving. At present, two promoters dominate the field—Semiphore Communications, which promotes "Ultimate Fighting," and Battlecade, which promotes "Extreme Fighting." Semiphore and

Battlecade are bitter rivals, and Donald Zuckerman (Battlecade's head of day-to-day operations) complained recently, "We've been very badly hurt by the way Ultimate Fighting has marketed itself, with statements like, 'This is a blood sport. Watch out! Somebody could die.'"

Under Battlecade's version of extreme fighting, a combatant can prevail in one of three ways—(1) his opponent is knocked out or choked out; (2) the opponent taps the canvas three times, indicating that he's had enough; or (3) the referee, the fight doctor, or a combatant's corner stops the fight. No biting, eye-gouging, elbows to the spine, or head-butting is allowed. However, combatants are permitted to punch to the groin. Originally, Battlecade's bouts consisted of one fifteen-minute round with a five-minute overtime. Now contests consist of three five-minute "phases" with a minute between rounds for rest.

Whereas Ultimate Fighting has no weight classes, Battlecade's Extreme Fighting has five. The three most marketable Extreme Fighting champions are Ralph Gracie (who hails from Brazil and now lives in Walnut Creek, California); Igor Zinoviev (a Russian immigrant residing in Brooklyn); and Maurice Smith (an American kick-boxing champion from Seattle). In the quest for greater visibility, Battlecade recently signed two men it hopes will become premier marquee attractions—Kenny Monday (who represented the United States as a freestyle wrestler at the last three Olympic Games, winning a gold medal in 1988); and Kevin Jackson (who won Olympic gold for America as a freestyle wrestler in 1992).

To date, Battlecade has promoted three nights of Extreme Fighting. The first was scheduled to take place at the Brooklyn Armory on November 18, 1995. But National Guard authorities cancelled the promoter's lease after a firestorm of protest, and the show was relocated on short notice to Wilmington, North Carolina.

The second card was held on a Kahnawake Indian Reservation in Quebec on April 26, 1996. "Four of our fighters were barred from the country by the Canadian government," Zuckerman recalls. "And on the day of the fights, the government sent faxes to all of our technicians, warning that they'd be arrested if they worked that night."

Battlecade's third card was showcased in Tulsa, Oklahoma, on October 18, 1996.

Subsequent to the bouts, both North Carolina and Oklahoma took legal steps to outlaw future mixed martial arts competitions on their soil. Quebec authorities made their point by arresting six fighters and three Battlecade officials the day after the fights. The charges are still pending.

That leads to an intriguing question: Extreme Fighting is often thought of in conjunction with tough-man competitions and spectacles like professional wrestling rather than professional boxing. Why?

The answer has many facets. First, extreme fighting doesn't have a tradition like boxing. One suspects that, if sumo wrestling were introduced today, it wouldn't be taken seriously either. Or phrased differently, if someone came up with the idea of having George Foreman bump bellies with Butterbean and charging people big money to watch, the inherent drama of the spectacle would not be readily apparent.

Second, the mainstream media refuses to take extreme fighting seriously—or publicize it.

Third, extreme fighting still suffers from an event that took place two decades ago. On June 25, 1976, the most famous night of mixed martial arts competition in history occurred.

For starters, Chuck Wepner did battle against Andre the Giant. "It was different to say the least," Wepner remembers. "Under the rules of the contest, if Andre grabbed me and I got to the ring ropes, then we were out of bounds and he had to let go of me. And there were certain rules that weren't made public at the time. I wasn't allowed to punch him in the face; only the body. And he wasn't allowed to take me down with kicks."

The bout ended when Andre, who was billed as 7 feet, 5-inches tall, 505 pounds, picked Wepner up and threw him out of the ring, and Wepner was disqualified for not getting back into the ring in time.

"I tried to resist, but he was just too strong," Wepner recalls. "He picked me up and threw me around like a feather. Still, I got $40,000 for it, which was more than I made for any of my regular fights except when I fought Ali. I also fought a bear twice," Wepner adds in closing, "and lost both times."

But if Chuck Wepner vs. Andre the Giant was bad, the nightcap was worse. Muhammad Ali took on Antonio Inoki in the main event that evening. For fifteen rounds, Inoki crab-walked around the ring on his rear end, horizontal to the canvas, kicking at Ali's legs. Ali threw six punches. Two of them, both jabs, landed. The bout was declared a draw.

But back to the present and the biggest problem extreme fighting has in gaining acceptance as a sport: It repulses people. The blood lust among extreme fighting crowds is more pronounced than at boxing matches, and the violence is less cosmetized. That might appeal to some fans, but it troubles others.

Still, the question remains: Will extreme fighting eventually gain more credibility than it has now?

Like it or not, boxing purists, the answer is probably "yes."

The sporting world is broadening its view of what is acceptable as "boxing." Women's bouts are now routine, and "tough man" contests are proliferating. Also, whether one likes extreme fighting or not, it has to be conceded that these are real athletes at work.

"If you're a fight fan and you start to learn about extreme fighting, you'll be impressed," says John Perretti, who serves both as matchmaker for Battlecade and TV commentator. "The sport features dozens of disciplines within disciplines. And the reality is that no one can compete successfully over time unless they're extremely skilled at finishing holds and ground fighting."

Also, as Zuckerman points out, "It's easier for the average guy to identify with our sport than with professional boxing. There are more than 15,000 martial arts dojos in the United States, and the number of gyms devoted to boxing is diminishing rapidly. Look at the movie business. Every few years, Hollywood produces one boxing movie, but there are dozens of martial arts films annually. And most people have never engaged in a fight with regular boxing rules. But at one time or another, even if it was only on the playground in grade school, virtually everyone has engaged in some form of extreme fighting."

Ultimately then, the success of mixed martial arts competitions will rest on marketing and how good the competitors really are. Zuckerman dreams of cross-discipline bouts matching his fighters against world-class boxers. Extreme fighting champ Ralph Gracie recently challenged Roy Jones to a bout, with Jones allegedly being offered $1,000,000 plus an additional million dollars for each minute he lasts against Gracie. How the promoters would bond the payment to Jones of $16,000,000 is open to question.

But competition between boxers and other martial arts combatants will never be the determining factor in how good extreme fighters really are. If the New York Yankees played baseball against a minor league British cricket team, the Yankees would win. But if it was cricket, the Brits would come out on top. The more interesting question is whether the combatants we're seeing now in extreme fighting are really the best in the world at what they do. At present, the talent pool isn't large enough to provide an answer.

Still, one would do well to consider the thoughts of Teddy Atlas, one of boxing's finest trainers. "I'm against extreme fighting for selfish reasons," Atlas says of the competition. "Its brutal aspects are so obvious that it gives more ammunition to people who want to ban boxing. But some of these guys are good. It's not just barroom brawling any more than professional boxing is just two guys slugging it out in a parking lot. Done right, extreme fighting is a skill. It's a test of technique and discipline. I was watching a fight a couple of months ago, and this guy was being choked. I mean, really choked by another guy who knew how to choke him. He didn't panic; he didn't succumb; he didn't give up. He got through it, and turned things around, and came back to win."

So who would win if someone like Mike Tyson fought Ralph Gracie or Igor Zinoviev?

"If they fight by Tyson's rules, obviously, Tyson knocks the other guy out easily," Atlas answers. "But if they fight by the other guy's rules, and the other guy gets by Tyson's punch—the next thing you know, he's got Tyson on the ground, and he's choking him. I don't know. I guess I've got to pick the other guy."

The easy availability of sports data online has diminished the need for print encyclopedias. Still, a tip of the hat to Sports Media Enterprises was in order.

Sport Magazine and Those Total Encyclopedias

Statistics are the lifeblood of sports. Few people remember more than one or two home runs that Hank Aaron hit, but they know he hit 755 of them. Wayne Gretzky rewrote hockey's record book. Wilt Chamberlain did the same for basketball. Meanwhile, at the other end of the spectrum, an obscure second baseman named Hutch Campbell has a degree of immortality because he played in two games for the Pittsburgh Pirates in 1907.

Sports legacies have many guardians. Wayne Parrish and Jim O'Leary are two of them.

Parrish and O'Leary have been friends since they were in their mid-twenties and met at the 1980 Winter Olympics in Lake Placid. At the time, they were reporters; Parrish for the *Montreal Gazette* and O'Leary for the *Toronto Sun*. Parrish subsequently changed employers and became general manager of the *Sun*. Meanwhile, O'Leary was named editor of the paper's Sunday edition and managed several of its online ventures.

In late 2000, Parrish and O'Leary left the newspaper business to found Sports Media Enterprises; a privately held corporation designed to create cross-media content in classic sports. Initially, they considered five areas of development: (1) books; (2) magazines; (3) documentary films; (4) high-end photography and sports memorabilia; and (5) Internet-based products. After two years of study, they decided to begin with publishing.

SME has made two significant acquisitions to date. First, it purchased the content and brand assets of *Sport* magazine. *Sport*'s inaugural issue was published in September 1946, and the magazine flourished for several decades with writers like Budd Schulberg, Grantland Rice, Jimmy Cannon, and Dick Schaap. It also pioneered the use of full-page full-color photography. But over time, *Sport* deteriorated. The August 2001 issue was its last.

The *Sport* archives include close to 250,000 photographs. SME now owns the copyright on many of them. Others can only be sold as single prints. SME also acquired rights to approximately 8,000 articles that appeared in the 648 issues of *Sport*.

The other acquisition was equally important. Early in its existence, SME made a secured investment in Total Sports, which had published several encyclopedias and, later, a line of books in conjunction with *Sports Illustrated*. In 2001, Total Sports went into bankruptcy. In 2002, SME purchased its assets at auction.

These two acquisitions are the now cornerstone of SME and its publishing imprint, Sport Classic Books.

At present, there are four "Total" encyclopedias.

Total Baseball, now in its seventh edition, is a massive 2,502-page tome. It's the "official" encyclopedia of Major League Baseball and has sold 325,000 copies to date.

Total Football (second edition) is the "official" NFL encyclopedia and weighs in at 1,652 pages.

Total Hockey, 1,974 pages, is also in its second edition and carries the official NHL designation.

Total Tennis was published earlier this year and, at 938 pages, is the runt of the litter.

Three more encyclopedias will be available shortly. The first edition of *Total Basketball* will go on sale this autumn. *Total Olympics* and *Total College Basketball* will be in bookstores in 2004. *Total Boxing, Total Golf,* and *Total Motor Racing* are on the drawing board.

"The core component of the encyclopedias is still the statistical reference material," says Parrish. "But what we're trying to do now more than in the past is put the statistics in context. That means surrounding them with well-written narratives and high-quality photographs."

As for books based on the *Sport* archives, two autumn 2003 releases are planned. *The Best of Sport* will be a collection of twenty-four articles matched with twenty-four full-color photographs; each one a profile of a major star in his prime. A second project, *The Italian Stallions,* will feature articles and photographs devoted to great Italian American fighters of the twentieth century.

"People associate *Sport* magazine with a better era," Parrish posits. "So far, we've only utilized the editorial content and photographs. But *Sport* is a good brand for a line of classic sports products, and we hope to do more in the future. The resonance is there."

Jerry Izenberg (once a contributor to *Sport*) concurs, saying, "The encyclopedias are superb reference books. And *Sport* was important. In its glory years, the magazine had great editors who gave writers freedom and a forum to say things that mattered. It was an authentic voice that brought out the best in us. In its golden era, *Sport* was golden."

An invincible champion; an overmatched foe. In 1997, I selected and revisited the ten greatest upsets of modern sports.

Upset ! ! !

Americans love upsets. Ever since George Washington coached the Continental Army to victory over England's top-ranked Big Red Machine, the nation has carried a soft spot in its heart for underdogs. Nowhere is that fondness more dearly held or more exuberantly expressed than in the world of sports.

An unexpected victory over college football's team of the moment will send an entire state into paroxysms of ecstasy. "The bigger they are, the harder they fall," has become an axiom of sporting faith. Moviegoers root unabashedly for Rocky, the Bad News Bears, and small-town basketball teams coached by Gene Hackman. Indeed, America's affinity for underdogs is such that Wilt Chamberlain once bemoaned his fate with the complaint, "Nobody roots for Goliath."

But if upsets were big news when David slew the mighty Philistine, they're bigger still in modern America. That's because sporting events are now seen, not by a select few, not on film, but as they unfold by tens of millions of people.

Some upset victories are flukes. Others signal the beginning of an extraordinary new reign. Some toppled champions come back. Others never recover. But one thing is clear. Television has given sports an immediacy and impact far beyond what anyone could have imagined forty years ago. And in the process, underdogs have become more popular than ever. So with eye on history, here's one person's view, in order, of the ten greatest upsets in modern times.

(1) James "Buster" Douglas vs. Mike Tyson (1990)

It didn't figure to be much of a fight; more like an execution than a competitive bout. In one corner, "Iron" Mike Tyson. The undisputed heavyweight champion of the world was undefeated in 37 bouts with 33 knockouts. At age twenty-three, he was considered by some to be the greatest fighter of all time.

Tyson was scary. There were suspicions that he needed to beat people up in order to sleep well at night, and sweet sayings like, "I tried to push the bone of his nose into his brain." Spectators came away from his fights with frightening images of Trevor Berbick reeling around the canvas, Larry Holmes going down like he was on roller skates, and Michael Spinks caving in. The man seemed invincible.

And in the other corner; James "Buster" Douglas, a twenty-nine-year-old journeyman from Columbus, Ohio. Douglas had been knocked out by David Bey and Mike White. Stefan Tangstad held him to a draw. His record was 29-4-1. And in addition to the specter of fighting Tyson, twenty-three days before the bout, Douglas had endured the death of his mother from a stroke. Most casinos wouldn't give odds on the fight. The few that did listed it at 40 to 1.

So Buster Douglas went out and knocked the crap out of Mike Tyson. He didn't just beat him; he beat him up. With the exception of ten seconds near the end of round eight when Tyson landed a crushing uppercut, the challenger thoroughly dominated the fight. In round ten, he knocked Tyson out. That's when another battle began.

For more than a decade, Don King had dominated boxing by controlling the heavyweight crown. First, Larry Holmes was his instrument of choice. Then it became a series of "alphabet soup" champions. And after that, Tyson. In order to fight for the heavyweight title, a challenger had to sign a promotional agreement giving Don King Productions three or more options on his services if he won.

Douglas had signed such a contract. But angered by King's postfight maneuvering (the promoter urged the WBC and WBA to strip the new champion of his title because of a phony "long-count" controversy), Douglas and his manager, John Johnson, refused to fight for King again. In the litigation that followed, King received a settlement of roughly four million dollars. But more significantly, instead of fighting a rematch with Tyson, Douglas defended against Evander Holyfield, who was backed by elements independent of King. Then Holyfield beat Douglas, and King's stranglehold over boxing's heavyweight division was broken.

What does Douglas think about his upset? "That's life," he says simply. "Sometimes the bully beats you, and sometimes you beat the bully."

(2) The Miracle Mets (1969)

The New York Mets were born in 1962 and promptly became base-ball's worst team ever. They lost 120 games and finished 57 games out of first place, dead last in a ten-team league. Four years later, they climbed to ninth, but sunk back to the cellar the following season. In 1968, there were signs of life as the team moved to within twenty-four games of the pennant-winning Cardinals. But that meant only that they were again in ninth place, sixteen games under .500.

The Mets were a symbol of ineptitude; baseball's longest-running joke. But in late 1969, the team caught fire, winning nineteen out of its final twenty-three regular-season games. That was enough to capture the National League's Eastern Division in the first year of League Champ-ionship Series play. Next, the Mets defeated Atlanta and moved into the World Series to face (gulp!) the Baltimore Orioles.

The Orioles were a dynasty in the making. In the course of nine years, they would win the World Series twice, capture four American League pennants, and engage in postseason play six times. Three members of the 1969 Orioles—Brooks Robinson, Frank Robinson, and Jim Palmer—were on the road to the Hall of Fame. Mike Cuellar was about to be named co-winner of the 1969 Cy Young Award. First baseman Boog Powell was a year away from being voted the American League MVP. The 1969 Orioles won 109 games. In all baseball history, only the 1906 Chicago Cubs, 1927 New York Yankees, and 1954 Cleveland Indians had won more.

Baltimore took a quick lead in Game 1 of the series when its lead-off hitter, Don Buford, hit the second pitch thrown to him for a home run. They scored three more times in the fourth inning, and triumphed 4 to 1.

Then the roof caved in. Donn Clendenon hit a home run in Game 2 as the Mets eked out a 2–1 win. Game 3 saw two Mets hurlers combine for a four-hit shutout en route to a 5–0 victory. In Game 4, Clendenon homered again; Ron Swoboda made a diving catch to rob Brooks Robinson of an extra-base hit; and the Mets prevailed 2–1 in ten innings. In Game 5, the Orioles took a 3–0 lead. But in the bottom of the sixth, Clendenon launched his third home run of the series; this time with a man on base. An inning later, Al Weis tied the score with his first home run ever at Shea Stadium. Two more runs followed in the bottom of the eighth. "The Miracle Mets" were world champions.

The Mets victory was sweet vindication for a city still smarting over the flight of the Dodgers and Giants to California a decade earlier. For Major League Baseball, it reaffirmed the view that new teams could be created and that they would be able to play competitively against old ones. That fact that 22 out of 27 players on the Mets roster had attended college was also a significant portent of baseball's future.

And, oh yes. It's worth mentioning that the Mets had a pretty good pitching staff. Led by a trio of third-year hurlers, they held Baltimore to a .146 World Series batting average. One of those third-year pitchers was Tom Seaver, who posted a 25-7 record that year. Another was Jerry Koosman, who won two games in the 1969 series. The third was a young reliever from Texas. Big fellow, good fastball, a little wild—Nolan Ryan.

In 1969, the all-time Major League career strikeout leader was Walter Johnson, who had struck out the seemingly unsurpassable total of 3,508 batters. By the time their respective careers were over, Ryan, Seaver and Koosman had *averaged* 3,970 strikeouts between them.

(3) Jets vs. Colts in Super Bowl III (1969)

"AFL-NFL World Championship Game III."

Sounds cumbersome, doesn't it? That's what Pete Rozelle thought. So after two previous confrontations, pro football's showcase game was officially renamed the "Super Bowl."

Except most people didn't think it would be very super. The Colts entered the game with a 15-1 record. During the previous ten weeks, they'd won ten in a row including four shutouts and held their opponents to seven touchdowns. When Johnny Unitas was struck down by injury, he'd been replaced at quarterback by Earl Morrall. All Morrall did was perform well enough to be voted NFL Player of the Year and lead Baltimore to a 34–0 triumph over Cleveland in the NFL title game.

Meanwhile, the Jets had struggled for much of the year, narrowly surviving Oakland in the playoffs. Because regular-season play between the leagues had yet to become a reality, the only sound basis for comparison between them were the two previous championship match-ups: Green

Bay 35-Kansas City 10, and Green Bay 33-Oakland 14. After the first of those victories, Packers coach Vince Lombardi had bluntly told a national television audience, "They [the Chiefs] don't even rate with the top teams in our division. There; that's what you wanted me to say, isn't it?"

The Colts were established as eighteen-point favorites over the Jets; the largest Super Bowl spread ever. But if the Jets were intimidated, they didn't show it. After the Super Bowl pairings were set, New York quarterback, Joe Namath, broke protocol by telling reporters that there were at least five quarterbacks in the AFL superior to Morrall. "Including me," Namath added. Then, at a luncheon several days before the game, he announced, "The Jets will win; I guarantee it."

Super Bowl III was becoming more than it game. It was shaping up as age versus youth; the establishment versus rebellion; flat-tops versus long hair. Vietnam and Aquarius colliding.

After a scoreless first quarter, New York went ahead 7–0 on a four-yard run by Matt Snell. Two third-period field goals by Jim Turner made it 13–0. With 13:26 left in the game, Turner's third field goal stretched the margin to sixteen. By then, Morrall had been replaced by Unitas, but to no avail. The Jets were too good. Final score: New York 16, Baltimore 7.

The AFL had come of age. And for those who thought that the Jets' victory was a fluke, a year later in Super Bowl IV, the AFL Kansas City Chiefs gave the Minnesota Vikings a 23–7 thrashing.

(4) United States Olympic Hockey Team (1980)

"The whole nation wanted this one," Mike Eruzione remembers. "The Soviet Union had invaded Afghanistan. Americans were being held hostage in Iran. The country was down. People everywhere were looking for pride. That's what made what we did so special."

But did anyone really think that the United States Olympic hockey team, captained by Eruzione, had a chance? The Olympic seeding committee didn't. It placed the Americans seventh in an eight-team draw. The public and media were equally skeptical. Sure, the United States had beaten the Soviets at Squaw Valley in 1960. But that was ancient history. Since then, the USSR had won four consecutive Olympic gold medals

and become *the* world power in hockey. The Soviets were better than the
pros. They'd crushed an NHL all-star team. Now some coach named
Herb Brooks was going to take a bunch of kids, average age twenty-two,
and beat the USSR with teamwork and plain old-fashioned hard work?
No way, Jose.

Want proof? Three days before the Olympics began, the Soviets
kicked "our boys'" butts all over the place in a 10–3 rout at Madison
Square Garden. Looking back, even Eruzione admits, "If we'd had to face
the Soviets at the start of the Olympics, things probably wouldn't have
gone as well as they did. But the way we played in our first few games at
Lake Placid, a positive feeling began to build."

Opening well was crucial. In their first game, the Americans earned a
2–2 tie with Sweden on a goal by Bill Baker with twenty-seven seconds
left on the clock. That was followed by a 7–3 drubbing of Czechoslovakia
and victories over Norway, Romania, and West Germany. Now, at least,
people knew the players' names.

Jim Craig was the goalie. Ken Morrow was the big defenseman. There
was Mark Pavelich, Neal Broten, Dave Christian, Rob McClanahan, Mark
Johnson. And the Soviets would annihilate them, but let's watch the tape-
delayed broadcast of the game on ABC anyway. And just to keep alive the
pretense that there's some doubt about the outcome, let's not listen to
news reports on television or radio beforehand.

Then came the game. The Soviets scored first and led 2–1 in the
waning moments of the first period. But with one second left on the
clock, Soviet goalie Vladislav Tretiak mishandled Christian's one-hundred-
foot slap shot and Johnson knotted the score off the rebound. Vladimir
Myshkin replaced Tretiak in the second period, which was dominated by
the Soviets. They outshot the Americans 12 to 2, and took a 3–2 lead that
stood up until 8:39 of the third period. Then, in the span of eighty-one
seconds, Johnson converted on a power play for his second goal of the
game and Eruzione sent a wrist shot through a screen, giving the United
States a 4–3 lead.

Bedlam . . . Delirium . . . The clock ticking down . . . Al Michaels
shouting, "Do you believe in miracles!"

Two days later, "our boys" did it again, beating Finland 4–2 for the
gold medal. That was accompanied by more images . . . Jim Craig gazing

into the crowd, asking, "Where's my father?" . . . Eruzione, summoning his teammates to the platform to join him for the medal presentation . . .

Did Team America have guts? Hey; in six of seven games, it gave up the first goal and came back to tie or win. Over the course of the Olympics, it was outscored 9 goals to 6 in the first period, but routed opponents 16 to 3 in the third.

"Strangers still come up to me on the street and tell me what a thrill we gave them," Eruzione says with satisfaction. "But the way the entire country got behind us, it was just as big a thrill for us."

Probably bigger. And "our boys" deserved it.

(5) Cassius Clay vs. Sonny Liston (1964)

Boxing was dying. The sport was at its nadir. Fight clubs were closing. And the heavyweight champion of the world was a mob-backed ex-convict named Sonny Liston, who radiated hostility and scorn. "A prizefight is like a cowboy movie," Liston once gloated. "There has to be a good guy and a bad guy. People pays their money to see me lose. Only, in my cowboy movie, the bad guy always wins."

Liston was regarded by many as the hardest punching heavyweight ever. The sole blot on his record was a 1954 loss to Marty Marshall, avenged by knockout seven months later. Thereafter, Liston improved dramatically as a fighter, winning and defending the championship by twice knocking out Floyd Patterson in the first round.

Cassius Clay, by contrast, was admired largely for his charm. Young, handsome, and a braggart beyond belief, Clay was considered by most "experts" to be cannon fodder for Liston; nothing more.

The champion entered the ring for their bout a 7 to 1 favorite. Then—

Cassius Clay "shook up the world." For three-and-a-half rounds, he dominated the fight with side-to-side movement and a lightening-fast jab. Liston was cut and appeared to be fading. The stage was set for the birth of a legend. But first came one of the great sports dramas of modern times.

At the end of round four, Clay started having trouble with his eyes. The most likely cause was an astringent that one of Liston's cornermen is believed to have rubbed on the champion's gloves. Regardless, Clay went back to his corner after the fourth round and told his trainer Angelo Dundee, "I can't see! My eyes! Cut the gloves off!"

"I pushed him down," Dundee remembers, "took a towel, and started cleaning out his eyes. Then I threw the towel away, grabbed a sponge, rinsed his eyes, and threw the sponge away. I only had a minute between rounds, and the referee was coming toward us to see what the problem was. Cassius was hollering, 'I can't see,' and I was scared they'd stop the fight. So I got his mouthpiece back in, stood him up, and said, 'This is the big one, daddy. Stay away from him. Run!'"

Clay survived round five by moving away and breaking Liston's concentration with jabs whenever the champion closed the gap between them. Then the challenger's vision cleared, he accelerated the pace, and Liston quit on his stool just before the start of round seven. It was an extraordinary moment; but as history attests, more extraordinary moments followed.

Two days after dethroning Sonny Liston, Cassius Clay announced that he had accepted the teachings of a black separatist religion known as the Nation of Islam. Thereafter, he changed his name to Muhammad Ali, refused induction into the United States Army during the height of the war in Vietnam, and continued to be what he wanted to be. Ultimately, he would become the most recognizable and most loved person in the world.

(6) Villanova vs. Georgetown (1985)

1985 was the year the NCAA basketball tournament expanded to sixty-four teams. It was also "The Year of The Big East." Georgetown, St. John's, Syracuse, Pittsburgh, Boston College, and Villanova each received invitations. Georgetown and St. John's were number-one regional seeds. And when all the games between the Mercers and Marshalls, Sweet Sixteens, and Elite Eights were over, the Final Four consisted of Memphis State and (trumpets please!)—Georgetown, St. John's, and Villanova.

Georgetown, the defending national champion, was awesome. Ranked number one, it had held opponents to 39.9 percent shooting, best in the country, during the regular season. Its center, Patrick Ewing, was the consensus choice as college basketball's Player of the Year. And just in case opponents weren't sufficiently intimidated, in their first five NCAA tournament games, the Hoyas held opposing teams to 51 points per game. Victim number five in that streak was St. John's, which lost by eighteen points to Ewing & Company in the semifinals when its own star, Chris Mullin, was held to single digits for the first time in 101 contests.

By contrast, Villanova entered the tournament with ten defeats, including two to Georgetown and a twenty-three-point loss to Pittsburgh in its final regular-season game. Unlike John Thompson, who had guided the Hoyas to three Final Four appearances in four years, Wildcats coach Rollie Massimino had never advanced past the regionals. Villanova hadn't been ranked in the top twenty all year. And while the Wildcats managed to beat everyone that the tournament organizers put in front of them, their performances were hardly scintillating. Indeed, during a semifinal win over Memphis State, Villanova's slowdown offense had more than a few fans chanting, "Boring! Boring!"

Villanova-Georgetown was far from boring. It was one of the most exciting encounters in college basketball history.

Taking advantage of the fact that the regular-season forty-five-second clock wasn't operative in tournament play, the Wildcats worked the ball around the perimeter and waited for high-percentage shots. Still, it seemed as though nothing they did could halt the Hoya juggernaut. Despite hitting seven of their first eight shots, the Wildcats trailed 20–14. They fought back, led by a point at halftime, and increased their lead to six points midway through the second half. Then Georgetown showed its strength, muscling its way to a 54–53 lead with 4:50 left to play. An eighteen-foot jump shot gave the lead back to Villanova. And in the final minutes, which seemed to last forever, eleven free throws under pressure sealed a 66–64 Wildcat win.

Villanova had played a near-perfect game. Against the best defensive team in the country, it had scored on 22 of 28 shots from the floor, including 9 of 10 in the second half. No loss ever hurt John Thompson more. And Rollie Massimino never had a bigger win.

(7) Secretariat Loses the Whitney Stakes (1973)

It was supposed to be a coronation. Instead, it became a reminder that in horse racing there's no such thing as a sure bet.

Secretariat was racing's first Triple Crown winner in twenty-five years. He'd won the Kentucky Derby and Preakness by 2 1/2 lengths each. Then, in the Belmont Stakes, the chestnut colt had put on the greatest performance in racing history, shattering Gallant Man's track record by 2 3/5 seconds, the equivalent of thirteen lengths. The closest competitor finished thirty-one lengths back.

Now, suddenly, Secretariat was more than a horse. He was a cultural phenomenon. The William Morris Agency was hired to license various rights. CBS made plans to televise the colt's next four races with Marlboro cigarettes as a special sponsor. Prior to the Kentucky Derby, a syndicate had paid $6,080,000 ($190,000 per share) for lifetime breeding rights to the horse. Immediately after the Belmont Stakes, Secretariat's owner, Penny Tweedy, turned down an offer of $450,000 for one share.

There was a carnival atmosphere in Saratoga, New York, as the Whitney Stakes approached. Three days before the race, five thousand people went to the track to watch Secretariat's 7:00 AM workout. Penny Tweedy, who owned the colt, became a celebrity in her own right. The horse had assumed an aura of invincibility.

But behind the scenes, trouble was brewing. For several days before the race, Secretariat had run a low-grade fever. Mrs. Tweedy later remembered, "On the day of the race, the fever was gone, and we thought the horse could run at his best. Lucien Laurin [Secretariat's trainer] and I made the decision together. It was a calculated risk. No one put any pressure on us. But the town of Saratoga had painted itself blue and white [Meadow Stable's colors], and I felt an obligation to have the horse perform. I was wrong; it was a mistake."

Secretariat went off as a 1-to-10 favorite before the largest crowd ever to watch a race at Saratoga. Only four other horses had been entered in the field. One of them, a four-year-old gelding named Onion, led every step of the way until the final turn where Secretariat drew even. Then Onion pulled away for his first stakes victory ever.

"It's embarrassing," Onion's owner, Jack Dreyfus, later reminisced. "I wish I could tell you I was there, but I wasn't. I knew Onion was running well, but I didn't think he'd beat Secretariat. So that afternoon, I was playing golf with Gary Player and my son at the Century Country Club in White Plains, New York. A couple of times, I thought about the race, but not with any real hope. Then, after we finished, I went back to the clubhouse, and someone told me, 'Onion beat Secretariat.' I was stunned."

So was Mrs. Tweedy. "I got a lot of letters after that race," she recalled. "Quite a few of them told me I was to blame; that it wasn't the horse's fault."

(8) Robert Shavlakadze over John Thomas at the Rome Olympics (1960)

Nineteen-year-old John Thomas was widely acclaimed as "the greatest high jumper in the history of mankind." Prior to the Olympics, he'd won fifty competitions in a row, including the Olympic Trials where he'd jumped 7 feet, 3 3/4 inches to shatter his own world mark. In the days leading up the competition in Rome, even the three-man Soviet high-jump contingent paid him homage by attending his public workouts. Each time Thomas sailed over the bar, the Soviets would gaze in wonderment. What Thomas didn't know was that the same Soviet jumpers were clearing seven feet regularly in secret practices. "I'd never heard of any of the Russian jumpers," he admitted later. "But in those days, who had? They didn't travel much."

It was the consummate "psych job." When the Olympic high jump competition finally began, Thomas was full of confidence. But as the day wore on, he became aware that, for the first time in years, he was competing against equals. The bar reached 7 feet, 1/4 inch. Thomas cleared it on his second attempt. Now he was alone in the field except for all three Russians. The bar was raised to 7 feet, 1 inch. Robert Shavlakadze, the lead Soviet jumper, cleared it on his first attempt. Teammate Valeri Brumel followed. Thomas missed on his first two tries. On his final attempt, he appeared to succeed. But his trailing leg brushed against the bar, sending it plummeting downward. Shavlakadze won the gold medal; Brumel the silver. Thomas was awarded third place on the basis of fewer misses than Viktor Bolshov, the third Soviet jumper.

The next four years were difficult for John Thomas. "I was the guy who'd lost to the Russians," he would say later. "In international sports, it was always the U.S. versus Russia; freedom versus communism; us versus them."

To make matters worse, Valeri Brumel soon emerged as the leading high jumper in the world, besting Thomas in eight out of nine competitions.

Then came the Tokyo Olympics. Now the roles were reversed. Brumel was considered a "cinch" for the gold. The prevailing view was that Thomas would be fortunate to win any medal at all.

The competition began. The field narrowed. Finally Brumel and Thomas were alone with the bar at 7 feet, 2 3/4 inches. Both men missed on their first two attempts. Brumel missed badly on his third try. Now John Thomas's fate rested on one jump. If he cleared the bar, the Olympic gold medal would be his. If not, Brumel would be awarded the prize on the basis of fewer misses at lower heights.

Thomas missed.

"I did my best," he told reporters afterward. "Even if I didn't satisfy anyone else, I satisfied myself and that's what counts."

Still, the hurt remained. And decades later, reflecting on the pressures that had been thrust upon him at an early age, Thomas would remark with a modicum of bitterness, "American spectators are frustrated athletes. They'd like to be champions but can't. So they sit and cheer the champion and ridicule the loser. In the champion, they see what they'd like to be. In the loser, they see what they actually are."

(9) Miami Beats Nebraska in the Orange Bowl (1984)

Nebraska was #1. The Cornhuskers had won twenty-two games in a row. Their offense, featuring Heisman Trophy winner Mike Rozier, was averaging 52 points and 545 yards per game. The line was anchored by Dean Steinkuhler, recipient of the Outland Trophy and Lombardi Award. It was a team for the ages; some thought the greatest college football team of all time.

Miami, by contrast, had been building from scratch. When coach Howard Schnellenberger arrived on campus in 1979, the Hurricanes had suffered through losing seasons in eight of the previous ten years. Their quarterback in the Orange Bowl was a redshirt freshman named Bernie Kosar, who looked Jewish, had been raised as a Catholic, and had a funny side-armed way of passing. True, the Miami defense was ranked fourth nationally in yards yielded per game and third in scoring defense. But Nebraska's offensive line outweighed the Hurricane defensive front by thirty-six pounds per man. The Cornhuskers were heavy favorites.

Miami came out sky-high. On their first possession, Kosar, completed three out of three passes on a fifty-seven-yard touchdown drive. Fifteen minutes into the game, the Hurricanes led 17–0.

But Nebraska came back strong. Steinkuhler scored on the Cornhuskers' version of a hidden-ball trick, picking up a deliberate fumble by quarterback Turner Gill and rumbling nineteen yards to the end zone. Then Gill tallied on a two-yard run. A thirty-four-yard field goal early in the third quarter knotted the game at seventeen all.

Miami had done its best. Now it was time for Nebraska to roll. Wrong.

Kosar led the Hurricanes to the Nebraska one, where Alonzo Highsmith took the ball in for a score. Then the 'Canes did it again.

With eleven minutes left on the clock, Nebraska trailed 31–17.

A seventy-six-yard Cornhusker drive narrowed the margin to 31–24. With 1:47 remaining in the game, Nebraska got the ball on its own twenty-six-yard line after a Miami field-goal attempt went wide. Inexorably, the Cornhuskers drove to the Miami twenty-four, where the Hurricane defense stiffened. Fourth and eight. Last chance. Gill pitched the ball to halfback Jeff Smith, who swept right and kept going into the Miami end zone. There were forty-eight seconds left on the clock. Nebraska trailed by one.

"I knew they'd go for two points," Schnellenberger reminisced later. "I also believed it was preordained that we'd win. I'd felt that way all along. The spirit in the Orange Bowl that night was electric. So many miraculous things had gone right for us that season. This was a game we were going to win. While Nebraska was getting ready for the conversion attempt, Kosar called our offensive team together on the sideline and was going over our two-minute drill. Whatever happened on that two-point play, the thought of losing just wasn't there."

Schnellenberger, who was huddling with his coaches, chose the right defensive formation. Gill's pass to Jeff Smith was batted away.

College football was never the same again. The Hurricanes were voted national champions. As college football's "team of the 1980s," they would earn that honor again in 1987, 1989, and 1991.

But in the process, there was another change. Soon, the Miami Hurricanes would be thought of as "heavies." Their image as underdogs had come to an end.

(10) Jack Fleck Bests Ben Hogan in the U.S. Open (1955)

Ben Hogan was king. In the world of professional golf, that was indisputable. In the eight years following World War II, he'd won four U.S. Open titles, two Masters, two PGA championships, and one British Open. He'd been named PGA Player of the Year four times. And for those who thought Hogan was getting old, in 1953 at age forty, he'd won the U.S. Open, Masters, and PGA crowns.

Jack Fleck operated two municipal golf courses located eight miles apart in Davenport, Iowa. He'd never placed better than sixth in a pro circuit tournament and shot a warm-up-round of 87 after qualifying for the 1955 U.S. Open. "All I really wanted to do," Fleck later remembered, "was finish in the top ten at the Open, so I wouldn't have to go through qualifying rounds to get into the tournament again the next year."

Hogan's goal was more ambitious. He wanted to win, which would place him on top of history's leaderboard with one more U.S. Open championship than the legendary Bobby Jones.

After two rounds, Hogan was positioned to achieve his goal. Tommy Bolt and Harvie Ward were tied for the lead with thirty-six-hole totals of 144. Hogan lay one shot back with Julius Boros and Walker Inman at 145.

Fleck was also at 145. He later reminisced, "At that point, I felt pretty good about it all. The course [at San Francisco's Olympic Club] had the heaviest rough of any U.S. Open course before or since, and I was a pretty accurate driver. I'm not saying I thought I'd win, but I was in love with the course. That's for sure."

In keeping with U.S. Open tradition, rounds three and four were played on the same day. Hogan took the tournament lead with a third-round 72 for a fifty-four-hole total of 217. Then, in round four, he pulled away from the field with a one-under-par 70 to finish at 287.

Meanwhile, Fleck fell behind with a third-round 75. And while he recovered nicely at the start of round four, a bogey on fourteen left him two strokes behind, with Hogan in the clubhouse and only four holes left to play.

Fleck birdied fifteen; then parred the next two holes. One hole left to play; one stroke behind.

The eighteenth hole was a 337-yard par four. On his first shot, Fleck played a three wood into the short rough. His second shot, a seven iron, landed seven feet to the right of the cup. On the green, Fleck took a single practice stroke, set his putter in front of the ball, then behind it, and stroked it in for a final-round 67.

An eighteen-hole playoff was scheduled for Sunday afternoon. Fleck was given little chance to win. He'd played four rounds over his head. Now, surely, Hogan would do him in.

Again, it came down to the eighteenth hole. Only this time, the two men were playing head-to-head, and it was Hogan who trailed by one. And Hogan folded. He double-bogied eighteen to finish at 72, and Fleck made his par for a three-stroke U.S. Open win. No one knew it at the time, but that was the closest Ben Hogan or anyone else would ever come to five U.S. Open triumphs. And it would be five years before Jack Fleck won on the pro tour again.

"Back then, people called it 'The Playoff of the Century,'" Fleck said years later, fondly looking back on that afternoon. "I know there have been other great playoffs since then. But it will always be 'The Playoff of the Century' as far as I'm concerned."

So there they are; the ten greatest upsets in modern sports.

There's room for argument. Cameroon's 1–0 soccer victory over Argentina in the 1990 World Cup meant as much to that tiny African nation as any Olympic hockey medal ever meant to the United States. When Dennis Conner's Liberty lost to Australia II in the 1983 America's Cup, it ended 132 years of American sailing dominance. The 1975 Golden State Warriors, led by Rick Barry, stunned the sports world with a 4-0 sweep of the Washington Bullets. And speaking of 4-0 sweeps, the 1954 New York Giants were pretty spectacular against the Cleveland Indians in a World Series that marked the emergence of Willie Mays on a national stage.

So let's raise a glass to all the "invincible" champions who've fallen and to the hopelessly overmatched underdogs who've prevailed. Upsets are the reason athletes run races, compete in fights, and play their timeless games.

When Larry Merchant turned seventy-five, I commemorated the occasion by writing about a little-known facet of his life: his exploits on the gridiron.

Larry Merchant: Play 42

This Saturday is a time of celebration. Larry Merchant, the heart and soul of HBO Boxing, will turn seventy-five. Merchant was born in New York on February 11, 1931. He's best known to sports fans for his association with the sweet science. But his first love was football, and he was pretty good on the gridiron.

In autumn 1947, Merchant was a sixteen-year-old senior at Lafayette High School, located in a working-class neighborhood near Coney Island in Brooklyn.

"We had a first-year coach named Harry Ostro," Merchant recalls. "He's still alive. He's in his nineties and lives in Georgia. Harry, which is what I call him now, played football at NYU and had been a captain in the airborne during World War II. He was a rugged barrel-chested guy; a prototypical coach, who believed in the homilies of the game. A winner never quits, and a quitter never wins. When the going gets tough, the tough get going. Vince Lombardi with a heart, is how I think of him. Harry led a lot of teenagers, myself included, from adolescence toward adulthood. He was an inspirational figure."

Lafayette football had a losing tradition. Ostro encouraged student-body support and built neighborhood pride in the team. He installed a single-wing offense and led the program to higher ground.

Merchant, at 5-feet, 7-inches, 155 pounds, was one of the mainstays of Ostro's first team. "I was fast," Larry says. "But our best player was Hal Seidenberg, who played tailback and later was a star running back at Cornell. I was the fullback, which meant I was mostly a blocking back. I ran the ball occasionally but not often. And I started on defense at what you'd call cornerback today. I was a good tackler and very good at analyzing plays as they unfolded. I had a knack for figuring out angles and where the ball was going."

The final game of the 1947 season was against Manual High School, a powerhouse from the Red Hook section of Brooklyn. Lafayette was undefeated. The game was at Ebbets Field, which was also where the Brooklyn Dodgers played. That afternoon, Merchant experienced the glory that sixteen-year-old boys dream of.

"Our left tackle, Vinnie Gargano, came back to the huddle and said we should run a play off the weak side," Larry remembers. "It was Play 42. That meant the position 4 back, who was Seidenberg, would run the ball through the number 2 hole, which was on the left side of the line between the tackle and end. But Seidenberg was winded so he said, 'Let Larry run it.'"

Merchant had never carried the ball on that play before; not in a game and not in practice. Ordinarily, his assignment on Play 42 was to block the defensive end. But this time, Lafayette ran it from the fullback position instead of tailback.

"The center snapped the ball to me instead of Seidenberg," Merchant recalls. "I don't think Seidenberg even blocked on the play. He just stood there, taking a rest, but the defense was keying on him. I took the snap, ran left, cut up field, and cut left again to the sideline. Nobody put a hand on me, and I outran everyone for a sixty-two-yard touchdown."

Jackie Robinson had just finished his rookie season in the major leagues. That year, he had played first base for the Dodgers. The way the gridiron at Ebbets Field was laid out, one end zone ran parallel to the wall in left field and the other was set against the first-base line.

"When I got to the end zone," Merchant recalls, "my first thought was, 'I've just scored a touchdown in Ebbets Field, and I'm standing where Jackie Robinson plays.'"

The final score was 19–19, which preserved the first undefeated season in Lafayette history. It was the only touchdown of Larry's high-school career.

Merchant graduated from Lafayette in January 1948 at age sixteen and enrolled at the University of Oklahoma. "How I got there is one of those mysteries of life," he says. "The Rodgers and Hammerstein musical *Oklahoma* had put the name in the air. Oklahoma had just come east to play the last of the great Army teams. I was a mid-year high-school graduate, and Oklahoma took mid-year graduates."

Oklahoma was quite a switch from Brooklyn. The state was seeking to erase its "Dust Bowl" image from the Great Depression. Indeed, John Steinbeck's monumental novel, *The Grapes of Wrath*, had been banned by several Oklahoma school districts. Meanwhile, Bud Wilkinson had just completed his first year as head coach of the Sooners with a 7-2-1 record. Ultimately, Wilkinson would become one of the most celebrated college coaches of all time. His teams captured national championships in 1950, 1955, and 1956, and amassed a 145-29-4 record prior to his retirement in 1963. The centerpiece of his reign was a forty-seven-game winning streak in the mid-1950s, an NCAA record that still stands.

"Wilkinson was like a god to a lot of people," Merchant says. "And it's easy to understand why. He was tall, extremely handsome, articulate, smart. And he won almost all the time."

Merchant tried out for the Oklahoma football team in 1948 as a spring-practice walk-on. "A lot of the players were World War II veterans in college on the GI Bill," he recalls. "I was a seventeen-year-old freshman, and they were men, quite a few of whom went on to play in the pros. When spring practice started, there were maybe 120 players. After five weeks, the number was down to around sixty. A lot of guys just couldn't take it and quit. I was dogged and stayed with it."

Darrell Royal, who later coached the Texas Longhorns to three national titles, played quarterback and halfback for the Sooners during Merchant's years at Oklahoma. Royal later recalled his peer as a tough little SOB and told Dan Jenkins of *Sports Illustrated*, "Larry would go after you."

Bud Wilkinson had a creed. If a player was willing to work hard every day in practice, he got a uniform. So in autumn 1948, Merchant was on Oklahoma's freshman team as a halfback and defensive back. That same year, the varsity went 10 and 1 and beat North Carolina in the Sugar Bowl. Larry was in the stands, watching, as the finale unfolded.

Merchant's sophomore season, he made the varsity. "I didn't get in a game," he remembers. "But one afternoon, Wilkinson called me into his office and told me, 'You're going to play a lot of football for Oklahoma.' That was one of the great moments in my life."

Then everything changed.

"Not long after that," Merchant says, "we were getting ready to play

Nebraska. I was on the scout team in practice, blocking on a sweep to the right. My shoulder hit the defensive end's knee, and I suffered a complete separation of the shoulder."

Sports medicine was very different in 1949 than it is today. Merchant's gridiron career was over. He never played football again.

Oklahoma went 11-0 that season and capped an undefeated campaign with a 35–0 rout of LSU in the Sugar Bowl. Merchant watched the bowl game in street clothes from the Sooner bench. "I spent most of the afternoon ogling the Kilgore Rangerettes, who were a precursor of today's Dallas Cowboys cheerleaders," he acknowledges. He also had dinner with one of the Rangerettes after the game."

And there's one final memory of the trip.

"Coming back on the train," Merchant remembers, I was reading *Moby Dick*. Wilkinson sat down next to me and asked what I was reading. He had a master's degree in English from Syracuse and knew his stuff. I told him and said, 'I'm having a problem; I can't understand the symbolism and imagery,' which was what we were discussing in English class. And Wilkinson told me in a very nice way, 'Don't worry; it's a great book. Just read it for a good story.'"

The following year, the Sooners rode a thirty-one-game winning streak into their third consecutive Sugar Bowl, where they lost 13–7 to a Kentucky team coached by Bear Bryant. By then, Merchant was sports editor for the school newspaper and watched from the press box. He graduated in August 1951, having risen to the position of editor-in-chief. Then he returned to Brooklyn, where he served on a part-time basis for three seasons as backfield coach for the Lafayette High School football team. Among other things, he instituted the split-T offense that he'd learned from Bud Wilkinson. "No one could stop us," he remembers. "We ran roughshod over the competition."

Thereafter, Merchant thought seriously about a career in coaching. "I'd been involved with a lot of successful teams," he says. "We were undefeated during my senior year of high school and also for two of the three years that I was the backfield coach at Lafayette. During my time at Oklahoma, the team lost only a few games. Harry Ostro and Bud Wilkinson were men I looked up to. I liked working with players and loved the chess-board aspect of the game."

"One memory from coaching stands out in my mind," Merchant continues. "The final game of my last season as backfield coach at Lafayette, we were playing Erasmus. Both teams were unbeaten, and whichever team won would be recognized as the best high-school football team in New York. Our quarterback was marching the team down the field. I was standing on the sideline next to the line coach. Before each play, I muttered to myself the play that I hoped the quarterback would call. This was before coaches sent in plays through substitutions, and the kid called virtually every play I muttered. The line coach even asked me, 'Are you calling the plays?' That's how eerie it was, and it was a transcendent moment for me. I realized that I had taught that kid how to play quarterback. The only reason I didn't go into coaching as a career was, at the high-school level, coaches also had to teach regular classes, and I didn't want to do that."

Later, as a journalist, Merchant wrote extensively about football. In 1977, he served as producer of NBC's Sunday-afternoon NFL studio program. But in recent years, his enthusiasm for the game has waned.

"I'm fascinated by the business side of football," he says. "And I'm amazed at how good the players are today. They're big and fast, far beyond anything in my day. But I don't watch football much anymore. The BCS Championship game, yes. The Super Bowl, absolutely. But for the most part, football bores me. And I'm appalled by the heightened brutality of the game, which is much worse now than when I played. Football is the most brutal sport I know. In terms of the battering that the body takes, it's far worse than boxing. And the injuries that football players sustain stay with them for their entire life. It's a killer game."

Then Merchant's voice softens. "I loved playing football," he says. "I loved the camaraderie and the competition. I always went all out. I liked going to practice every day. I'm glad I had the experience of playing football. There was a time when it was an important part of my life."

Sports Illustrated's choice for "Sportsman of the Year" is always analyzed and debated. In 2008, I took the process one step further.

Black and White and *Sports Illustrated*'s "Sportsman of the Year"

Each year since 1954, *Sports Illustrated* has honored a "Sportsman of the Year." As defined by the magazine, the award is bestowed upon "the athlete or team whose performance that year most embodies the spirit of sportsmanship and achievement."

This year's honoree is Michael Phelps. I don't question his credentials. He's a superb competitor and a true sportsman. But his selection raises a nagging question. Over the decades, have the editors of *Sports Illustrated* leaned toward white athletes in choosing their "Sportsman of the Year"?

Let's start with some numbers.

There has been a single honoree in forty-four of the fifty-five years that the award has been given. Ten of the single honorees were black; thirty-four were white.

In seven years, there have been dual honorees. In three instances, both honorees were white. Once, they were both black. On three occasions, there was a racial mix.

In 1987, the magazine honored eight athletes for their involvement in community work. Four of the eight were black.

Over the course of fifty-five years, there have been forty-seven white honorees, nineteen black honorees, and three teams. One of the teams was all white; one had a single black player; the third was predominantly white.

Sports Illustrated has been in the vanguard of those fighting for racial justice in sports. In the 1960s, it took the lead in reporting on the plight of black athletes. It was supportive of Muhammad Ali's right to practice his religion as he saw fit when many media giants took a contrary view. It's a wonderful magazine.

But given black America's dominance in sports over the past half-century, one might question whether an unintended racial bias has crept into the magazine's "Sportsman of the Year" selection process. And that question is particularly appropriate given the fact that, on several occasions, *Sports Illustrated* indicated that the award was being bestowed for lifetime achievement as much as for the recipient's accomplishments in a single year. And each of these recipients (Jack Nicklaus, Don Shula, Cal Ripken Jr., Dean Smith, and Bret Favre) was white.

Weren't Willie Mays, Hank Aaron, Roberto Clemente, Wilt Chamberlain, Oscar Robertson, Walter Payton, and Eddie Robinson equally deserving?

Just asking.

Sports Illustrated's "Sportsman of the Year" Honorees

1954	Roger Bannister
1955	Johnny Podres
1956	Bobby Joe Morrow
1957	Stan Musial
1958	Rafer Johnson
1959	Ingemar Johansson
1960	Arnold Palmer
1961	Jerry Lucas
1962	Terry Baker
1963	Pete Rozelle
1964	Ken Venturi
1965	Sandy Koufax
1966	Jim Ryun
1967	Carl Yastrzemski
1968	Bill Russell
1969	Tom Seaver
1970	Bobby Orr
1971	Lee Trevino
1972	Billie Jean King
	John Wooden
1973	Jackie Stewart
1974	Muhammad Ali

1975	Pete Rose
1976	Chris Evert
1977	Steve Cauthen
1978	Jack Nicklaus
1979	Terry Bradshaw
	Willie Stargell
1980	U.S. Olympic Hockey Team
1981	Sugar Ray Leonard
1982	Wayne Gretzky
1983	Mary Decker
1984	Edwin Moses
	Mary Lou Retton
1985	Kareem Abdul-Jabbar
1986	Joe Paterno
1987	Bob Bourne
	Judi Brown King
	Kip Keino
	Dale Murphy
	Chip Rives
	Patty Sheehan
	Rory Sparrow
	Reggie Williams
1988	Orel Hershiser
1989	Greg LeMond
1990	Joe Montana
1991	Michael Jordan
1992	Arthur Ashe
1993	Don Shula
1994	Bonnie Blair
	Johann Olav Koss
1995	Cal Ripken Jr.
1996	Tiger Woods
1997	Dean Smith
1998	Mark McGwire
	Sammy Sosa
1999	U.S. Women's World Cup Soccer Team

2000	Tiger Woods
2001	Curt Schilling
	Randy Johnson
2002	Lance Armstrong
2003	David Robinson
	Tim Duncan
2004	Boston Red Sox
2005	Tom Brady
2006	Dwyane Wade
2007	Bret Favre
2008	Michael Phelps

*There are a lot of "feel-good" stories in college sports. This one was
"feel-bad."*

Hypocrisy at West Point

Caleb Campbell (United States Military Academy, class of 2008) is
twenty-three years old and was captain of the 2007 Army football team.
Less admirably, he is a prime example of the hypocrisy that attends the
war currently being waged at the behest of his commander in chief.

Virtually all of Campbell's classmates will be serving in Iraq or
Afghanistan by the end of this year. That's in keeping with the requirement that West Point cadets commit to five years of active military duty
in return for their education.

Students at the Naval and Air Force academies incur a similar obligation. Roger Staubach spent four years in the Navy (including a tour of
duty in Vietnam) before beginning his Hall of Fame career with the Dallas
Cowboys. David Robinson also served on active naval duty before achiev-
ing superstar status with the San Antonio Spurs. Air Force Academy graduate Chad Hennings was on active duty in his branch of the service
before playing in the National Football League.

This obligation, shared by young men and women at the service
academies, is a bond that transcends the normal ties between student athletes. Cadets do more than play on the same team; they have a common
future. Seniors in the Army-Navy football game know that they're competing with and against each other for the last time before serving in
common cause.

However, in March 2005, the United States Military Academy
adopted an "Alternative Service Option" for athletes. This program
releases cadets who have "unique talents and abilities" (i.e. are good enough
to play in a major professional sports league) from their commitment to
serve five years of active duty in the Army. In return, the cadet must, for
two years, "participate in activities with potential recruiting or public
affairs benefit to the Army" at the same time he's pursuing his pro sports

career. He may then erase the remaining three years of his active-duty commitment by serving in the Army Reserve.

In other words, if Caleb Campbell makes a National Football League roster, rather than risk his life in Iraq or Afghanistan, he can speak to young people and seek to recruit them to serve in his stead.

The purpose of the "Alternative Service Option" was to resurrect the football program at West Point. In the five years prior to its adoption, Army's gridiron record was a pitiful 5 wins and 53 losses. Coaches at West Point can now recruit elite high-school athletes with the sales pitch, "Come to West Point. If you're good enough to play in the NFL, you can avoid military combat."

That's a far cry from World War II and the Korean War, when the United States asked great athletes like Ted Williams to serve in the armed forces alongside everyone else.

The most disturbing aspect of all this is the light it sheds on our priorities as a nation. The United States Military Academy is, in effect, saying that it considers entertaining sports fans to be more important than the war in Iraq. How else can one construe giving a young man the choice of (a) living up to his commitment to serve his country or (b) playing in the National Football League?

The situation calls to mind another young man of exceptional promise. Pat Tillman graduated summa cum laude from Arizona State University in 1998 and was drafted by the Arizona Cardinals of the National Football League. He became the team's starting safety and, in his third year as a pro, broke the franchise record for tackles in a single season.

One day after 9/11, Tillman told an interviewer, "At times like this, you stop and think about just how good we have it, what kind of system we live in and the freedoms we're allowed. A lot of my family has gone and fought in wars, and I really haven't done a damn thing."

Then Tillman did something extraordinary. He turned down a $3,600,000 contract extension from the Cardinals, put his football career on hold, and enlisted for a three-year term in the U.S. Army. He served in Iraq and then in Afghanistan. On April 22, 2004, he was killed in action.

Pat Tillman's memory is dishonored by West Point's "Alternative Service Option." Perhaps the United States Military Academy should change its motto from "Duty, Honor, Country," to "Evade, Avoid, NFL."

As for Caleb Campbell; if he accepts the forbidden fruit that the Army is offering, one can imagine the recruiting pitch that he'll make to young men and women: "I wasn't willing to risk my life in Iraq and Afghanistan, but you should."

The outpouring of mail I received in response to "Hypocrisy at West Point" led to this follow-up column.

West Point Revisited

Earlier this month, I wrote an article entitled "Hypocrisy at West Point" that called into question a policy known as the "Alternative Service Option." In relevant part, that policy states, "Army cadet-athletes now have options to pursue professional athletic opportunities thanks to the U.S. Army's "Alternative Service Option" program. If cadet athletes are accepted into the program, they will owe two years of active service in the Army, during which time they will be allowed to play their sport in the player-development systems of their respective organizations and assigned to recruiting stations."

In other words, a West Point graduate sufficiently skilled to play professional sports can pursue his athletic career without interruption. As a trade-off, he must recruit other young men and women to enter the military and face the risks inherent in combat that he has not faced.

Since the "Alternative Service Option" was inaugurated in 2005, six cadets have sought to exercise it. The spotlight is currently on Caleb Campbell, who captained the 2007 Army football team and has pro potential. Recently, Campbell told the *Dallas Morning News*, "I think this is a great opportunity to get all-star kids into the academy, because they'll know they still have a chance to play football after they leave the academy. Some [NFL] teams wanted to know if I'd be able to play for sure. They wanted to know if I'd have to go to Iraq if I got called up. Do we invest all kinds of money in a player just to let him go? Now all the teams have the understanding I can play football. My duty right now is to play football."

"Hypocrisy at West Point" engendered a remarkable response. On the day it was posted, I received more than one hundred emails, the overwhelming majority of them from graduates of West Point and Annapolis. I also heard from the parents of quite a few young men and women now serving in the military and graduates of the Air Force Academy. Writing about the "Alternative Service Option" has turned into a rewarding experience for me, in large part because of the dialogue I've had with so many graduates of the service academies and their families.

The Annapolis alumni who wrote to me were close to unanimous in opposing the alternative service option. A majority of West Point graduates also disliked the program.

Many of the correspondents had questions about my own background and beliefs, so here's a thumbnail sketch.

I'm sixty-two years old. I attended college and law school at Columbia. In 1967 (after antiwar protests led the school administration to cancel an invitation to the United States Army to recruit on campus), I invited the Army to recruit at Columbia in my role as president of the graduating class. Although I thought the war in Vietnam was wrong, I believed (and still do) that a strong military is essential to our national security.

I was a practicing attorney for six years. Then I turned to writing.

I consider myself a liberal on social issues, moderate with regard to foreign policy, and an economic conservative. I don't think that "conservative" means letting financial institutions run wild, running up hundreds of billions of dollars in budget deficits, and cutting taxes for rich people in a time of war.

I believe that there is a place where the values of well-intentioned people with different mindsets coincide.

I did not serve in the military. I've always respected the military and understand that, properly employed, it safeguards our democratic way of life. The young men and women who attend the service academies have unique motivation and talents. The defense of our country is in their hands.

I have no reason to question Caleb Cambell's character. He's following the rules as he found them. I have a problem with the rules. It's precisely because I understand how important the United States Military Academy is that I'm troubled by the "Alternative Service Option."

I'm also troubled by the fact that the current administration hasn't asked the American people as a whole (and particularly wealthy Americans) to make greater sacrifices in a time of war. The war in Iraq is being conducted in a manner that ensures it won't interfere with our fun and games. Perhaps there's a fear that, if the American people are called upon to sacrifice, we won't support the war. Or worse; perhaps we'll vote the people who led our country into the war out of office.

If a war is just, the American people will sacrifice to support it. If it isn't just, it shouldn't be fought.

There's nothing brave about middle-aged politicians who have never seen combat sending other people's children to die in battle. I believe that the civilian architects of the war in Iraq are reckless with other people's lives and owe an apology to the men and women in our armed forces who they have needlessly put in harm's way.

I also believe that the best way to support the men and women currently serving in our armed forces in Iraq is to bring them home as quickly and safely as possible.

Several hours after "Hypocrisy at West Point" was posted, the director of communications for the West Point Association of Graduates distributed a memorandum to a number of association members entitled "Alternative Service Option Talking Points." Recipients of the memo were advised to say, "These young Soldiers are still serving their country, just in a different way."

Another "talking point" read, "Just a few weeks ago, the *Seattle Times* had a long glowing article on Seattle Mariners pitching prospect, 2LT Nick Hill (USMA 2007). The article focused not on Nick's pitching but on the Army and on West Point. Circulation? 220,000. And how much would it cost for us to buy that many column inches in the Seattle Times? $63,000."

Judging from the emails I received from United States Military Academy graduates, they weren't impressed by the talking points. "Just think of all the column inches Roger Staubach could have gotten if he'd gone directly from Annapolis to the NFL," one West Point graduate wrote. "Of course, the column inches he got had special meaning after he'd fulfilled his commitment to serve."

The "proud mom" of a young woman currently at Annapolis referenced the famous World War II declaration by Army Chief of Staff General George C. Marshall ("I need an officer for a secret and dangerous mission. Send me an Army football player") and asked, "What happened to 'send me an Army football player'? I guess the new response is, 'Sorry, he's in the NFL; but we do have Navy and Air Force football players who will do the job, sir.'"

The column spurred discussion and debate. I think that's good. And I was impressed by the nature of the emails I received. Whether or not the correspondents agreed with me, they expressed themselves in a well-thought-out manner. Rather than speak for them, I'd like to let them speak for themselves.

The following is a representative sample of views communicated to me by men and women who have attended West Point and Annapolis, their families, and others who've served in the armed forces:

★ With a son at the Academy who insists on the Marine Corps at graduation, I am stunned that the Army will allow cadets to avoid "real" military service in order to play football. Granted, Army has been defeated by Navy year after year. However, attending any military academy is a serious commitment to one's country; not a potential NFL contract.

★ Some academically gifted Academy graduates go directly to graduate school for advanced degrees; some go directly to medical school; some go to Olympic team training; some are found not physically qualified for a commission. On rare occasion, there is an exceptional graduate from a service academy who is good enough to try out for a major professional sports team. These individuals can and usually do great recruiting service for their country while pursuing their dreams.

★ The service academies turn down thousands of qualified applicants each year. Caleb Campbell took a spot at West Point that could have been filled by another young man or woman anxious to serve in the United States military to the fullest extent possible.

★ Is the next step a lowering of standards to admit talented athletes who would not otherwise qualify for admission to West Point? And if so, what sort of military leaders will these young men and women make?

★ I have two sons who earned varsity letters at West Point, though in a sport that does not offer lucrative professional contracts. Both are now serving on active duty. Both have deployed to Iraq and are likely to do so again. If anybody would resent the very few baseball, football, and basketball players and other cadets who have explored the Alternative Service Option, you would think it would be West Point graduates like my sons, their classmates, and their teammates. Yet I have never heard such resentment expressed by any of them. Or resentment toward the several West Point athletes who, as active serving officers, are tasked to train for the Olympics. They believe that all of these soldiers serve in their way.

★ I would not have gone pro while my classmates were putting their lives on the line.

★ All service is honorable. Combat service is not inherently more valuable or honorable than recruiting duty, public affairs officer work, staff work in the Pentagon, or overnight gate guard duty at Fort Hood, Texas. To imply otherwise is to denigrate the service of those who, for one reason or another, do not get deployed.

★ Last year, a Navy Lieutenant who was serving at the United States Naval Academy and was a former USNA baseball player had a brother who was an enlisted soldier in the Army and was on his way to Iraq for the third time. He had a question. "Why does the Army let their officers from West Point out of their commitment to serve and my brother has to go back there for a third time?"

★ At most colleges, when a football tradition falters, rich alumni pressure the school to upgrade the football program at any cost. At West Point, we have a tradition that's more important than football.

★ I would challenge you to look at the bigger picture and the broader impact West Point has on this great country of ours. Having a strong athletic program is a big part of that impact. It serves to unite those of us who have graduated and boosts our morale when we are deployed.

★ As a graduate of the Naval Academy, I agree with your article in its entirety. As nice as it might seem to be able to leave school and go to a lucrative pro football career, that is not the purpose of these institutions. Navy is continuing to abide by the requirements all recruits know about when they enter the school. I am proud that they intend to continue this tradition.

★ I love college football. I particularly love Navy football. I admire and appreciate those young men and how hard they work to live their dream. Sure, they have more than average ability but their achievements are gained mostly through exceptionally hard work and sacrifice. These are the men I want fighting with and for me. When their teams are successful, they encourage younger high achievers of all skills and talents to attend the Academies. High achievers do not want to be associated with losers. The goal is to produce great leaders, and I think winning NCAA Division I football supports that goal.

★ When Caleb Campbell is "on duty" in the National Football League, will he be paid what other NFL players are paid or Army wages?

★ These kids that go to the Academies need to realize and acknowledge that they go to an Academy to become an officer in the military; not to perhaps get a chance to play pro ball.

★ I am in total agreement with you. However, there is a point that needs to be mentioned. The West Point cadet at the end of two years at West Point has no service obligation. He/she can decide at that point to leave with no pay-back or service commitment, athlete or not. The issue as I see it, is; cadet decides to stay and signs commitment papers for the last two years. He made the choice and the Government paid for his education. I believe the signing obligates the cadet to the five years of active duty. He had a choice to leave before he signed and did not. If you go to one of the service academies and, after two years, are athletically talented enough to move on, leave. Do not suck up the taxpayers money for the last two years with no intention of serving on active duty while you get a degree from one of the top colleges in the United States completely funded.

★ The current saying that "The military is at war; America is at the mall," goes to the heart of the issue.

★ The decision to offer the Alternative Service Option was made at very senior levels in the Army. Unlike you and I, these general officers are responsible for the accomplishment of the Academy's mission. Every day, they balance competing priorities and resource constraints to meet the needs of the Army for a new class of West Point graduate lieutenants each May. Inspiring the best and brightest young Americans to seek an appointment to the Academy is part of that mission. If it takes a successful football program to do that, then so be it.

★ The Alternative Service Option isn't about recruiting for the Army. It's about recruiting for the Army football team.

★ There are some of us who don't think it's appropriate for a graduate of West Point to spend his active duty years playing baseball or football. What's the point of a West Point education if it isn't put to use the way it was intended?

★ Thanks for reminding me of Pat Tillman. Thumbs down to an institution I respect.

★ I am a graduate of the US Naval Academy and served my five year obligated service in the US Marine Corps. I was also a varsity football player for the academy. Do you have any idea of the impact that a winning academy sports team (particularly football) has on the morale of the rank and file service man/woman? Do you understand the impact that winning sports teams have on attracting the very best candidates to the academies? There is a great deal of good that can come from resurrecting the West Point football program.

★ I commend you for stating the issue so clearly. Many of us are concerned about the way in which the current leadership of our military seems to have lost sight of the intangible moral honorable side of the education the academies provide.

★ It would be interesting if all of the service academies published data comparing the in-school performance, graduation rate, and post-graduation military assignments of their elite athletes. It's not just the USMA that should be questioned. Take a closer look at the Air Force Academy.

★ David Robinson was 6-7 when he entered Annapolis and 7-1 when he left. He simply was too large to be stationed on navy ships or to be a Marine. He had an opportunity to leave school at the end of the first semester of his junior year, but elected to stay and complete his degree under an arrangement in which he served two years (on active duty) followed by an extended six-year reserve obligation. Nobody, with the possible exception of Roger Staubach (who served four years on active duty) could have been a better ambassador for our school than he has been.

★ I did thirty years in the Army and now live in the Annapolis area and am very disappointed with the Army position. Just so they can beat Navy in a football game. Seems we have lost more than just a game.

★ After Pearl Harbor, the commissioner of baseball wrote to Franklin Roosevelt and asked whether baseball should continue to be played during the war. Roosevelt wrote back that it should, but warned that many of baseball's best players would be drafted. The Army says that Caleb Campbell can serve as a poster boy for military recruiting. Ted Williams served as a different kind of poster boy.

★ And they still cannot beat Navy.

A lot of thought went into the views expressed above. I want to add one last thought of my own to them.

My previous article contained a reference to the United States Military Academy motto: "Duty, Honor, Country."

General Douglas MacArthur, in his Farewell Speech to the Corps of Cadets at West Point, referred to "those three hallowed words" as "an expression of the ethics of the American soldier" and "a great moral code."

The reference I made to the motto was disrespectful and inappropriate. I apologize for it.

Tim McCarver is one of the most articulate, knowledgeable, likeable men in sports. It was a pleasure to talk with him at the start of the 1999 baseball season.

Tim McCarver

Tim McCarver, the son of a policeman, was born and raised in Memphis. He was a multi-sport athlete in high school, and received football scholarship offers from dozens of colleges, including Notre Dame, Alabama, Kentucky, and Tennessee. After graduating from high school, he signed with the St. Louis Cardinals and made his major league debut in 1959 at age seventeen.

Over twenty-one seasons as a major-league catcher, McCarver developed a reputation as a fierce competitor. He was quick behind the plate, and his instinct for the game, combined with careful study, made him one of baseball's most reliable catchers.

The high point of McCarver's major league career was the 1964 World Series, when the Cardinals beat the New York Yankees four games to three. McCarver caught every game, had 11 hits in 23 at bats, and blasted a three-run eleventh-inning home run that gave the Cards a 5–2 victory in the pivotal fifth game. He is the only catcher ever to lead the major leagues in triples, with thirteen in 1966. And he finished second in the 1967 National League Most Valuable Player balloting behind teammate Orlando Cepeda.

Perhaps more significantly in the overall fabric of sports, McCarver was one of a small group of players who helped reorganize the Major League Baseball Players Union in 1966 and choose Marvin Miller as its executive director. Thereafter, he was a member of the players negotiating committee that secured baseball's first basic collective bargaining agreement.

After retiring from the game as an active player in 1980, McCarver took a job as a TV commentator for the Philadelphia Phillies. Three years later, he brought his skills in the broadcast booth to the New York Mets. At the same time, he went national, calling games for CBS, ABC, and now Fox.

Earlier this year, McCarver's services were terminated by the Mets. Clearly, he ranked among the sports broadcasting elite. But his honest commentary and occasional criticism did not sit well with Mets management. A firestorm of controversy followed. The Mets were savaged by fans and the media. And McCarver was quickly signed to provide analysis for 42 of 50 Yankee games that will be televised by Fox's local affiliate in New York. Meanwhile, McCarver remains a member of Fox's broadcast team for national telecasts. And he remains both outspoken and candid.

Q: How did you feel when you were terminated by the Mets?

McCarver: I tried to view it from a business standpoint. Changes are made in corporations everyday. And from a personal standpoint, I told myself that change in life can be healthy and for the best. There were people in the Mets organization who thought I was overly critical for a local announcer. And if that filtered up—down, over, whatever—to the owners, then it was time for them to make a change and time for me to move on. I was surprised, and a little angry initially, but that's gone now.

Q: How involved was George Steinbrenner in your hiring by the Yankees? And how do you think he'll react if you criticize him?

McCarver: There's no question in my mind that George had to give his okay before I was accepted in the Yankee booth. But I never met with him in conjunction with the job before my contract was signed. As for the second part of your question; I was amused to read where George said, "Yeah, McCarver has taken a few shots at me in the past, but it will be all right as long as he's fair." Now to George, it may be taking a few shots. To me, it's balanced criticism. And that's the way I'll try to be as long as I'm on the air. The only time I can remember criticizing George on a national stage was in Game 4 of the 1996 World Series. Kenny Rogers, the starting pitcher for the Yankees, was taken out in the third inning with Atlanta leading 6 to 0. And I said something to the effect that George Steinbrenner should be given a lot of credit for what he'd done with Darryl Strawberry and Doc Gooden, but that he'd been wrong in insisting that the Yankees acquire Rogers over the objections of Joe Torre and

Bob Watson, both of whom had wanted to sign Chuck Finley as a free agent. I know for a fact that George was very upset about that comment.

Q: What is your philosophy of broadcasting?

McCarver: Fairness. A good broadcast is tough on players when it needs to be and glowing about players when they deserve it. If a fellow is hitting .220, there's no way to put a glossy bent on that. He's not doing his job. Now if you make a comment like that, you might ruffle a few feathers. But if you don't make a comment like that, then you're not doing your own job because you have a responsibility to viewers to tell the truth. Also, your role changes depending on how a game is going. In an 11 to 1 ballgame, you have to be more of an entertainer than a reporter because— let's face it—if it's 11 to 1 in the eighth inning, the game is over.

Q: Who are your favorite TV sports announcers?

McCarver: Al Michaels is probably my favorite play-by-play guy. With Al, you always know what the situation is. He's so clear in the way he broadcasts. There's virtually no hint of bias. He has an underappreciated sense of humor. I worked with Al, and learned far more from him than I learned from anybody else about the business of broadcasting, the mechanics of broadcasting, timing, rhythm, cadence, how to use the monitor, the way to interact with your partner, making a broadcast seamless; all of the things that are so important.

Q: Anybody else?

McCarver: From an analyst's standpoint, I'm a huge admirer of John Madden. And there are others. Walt Frazier, Dick Stockton, Jim Kaat, and John McEnroe are four who come to mind. I thought Howard Cosell was good in his early years. He added a great degree of candor to the business; the freedom to speak one's mind. But it was unsettling in Howard's later years, when he began taking shots at everybody for no good reason. That's how I got my first job in post-season play; in 1985, when Howard was fired. But he had a huge positive impact on the world of broadcasting.

Q: Would you like to try your hand at announcing other sports?

McCarver: I don't think so. I did the Olympics in 1992 and enjoyed it immensely. But to do football or any other sport, from an analytical standpoint, I don't think I could add anything. My credibility lies with baseball. At this point in my life, that's where I'd prefer to remain.

Q: Have sports been blown out of perspective in today's society?

McCarver: No. I think it's healthy for people to live vicariously through their sports heroes. It might become overly obsessive with some people. But I'm not one who believes that sports play too big a role in our society. I think they play a constructive, and maybe even a necessary, role.

Q: What obligations do athletes have to fans and the media?

McCarver: Frank Sinatra once said, "The only thing you owe the public is a good performance." An athlete certainly owes the public that. But from a responsible business standpoint and a responsible human standpoint, I think something more is involved. The public can be very demanding. Everybody realizes that. But the smart athletes know how to handle it. Also, I find it amusing that baseball is the only major sport where players in uniform are asked to sign autographs. You'd think it was farcical if someone ran down to the football field and asked Terrell Davis for his autograph while the Denver Broncos were warming up. Or Shaquille O'Neal or Wayne Gretzky during warm-up time. But it's one of the charms of baseball that, five minutes before a game, you see fans leaning over the railing, asking for autographs. And a lot of players accommodate them.

Q: Compared with the rest of the population, are baseball players happy?

McCarver: For the most part, I think they are. You're playing a little boys game. That helps perpetuate youth; and anything that perpetuates youth gives you an advantage in being happy. It's the transition period, when you retire from baseball, when the problems set in. Making that transition to everyday life is very hard. Those who do it successfully are usually the ones who are very intelligent and have prepared in advance for that time in their life.

Q: What's it like to be traded from one team to another?

McCarver: Very difficult. On an emotional scale, the initial trade is the most damaging. An organization signs you, trains you; and throughout the whole process, it tells you that you're part of a family. After a while, you start to believe it, so that first trade is very hard. I don't think any professional experience I have will ever equal the emotional depths I felt when I was traded from the Cardinals in 1969. Then you become hardened to it. You never get used to it, but it becomes less hurtful after two or three times, particularly in this era of free agency. And it should be emotional. You have a connection with your teammates and you have a connection with the fans who have seen you for so many years.

Q: How did you feel about the 1998 NBA lockout?

McCarver: That's not my bailiwick anymore; I only follow sports labor negotiations peripherally. But I thought it was a huge victory for ownership over the players. And I was very surprised at the apathy of basketball fans compared to baseball fans. If you compare the two labor disputes—baseball in 1994 and basketball in 1998—there was a tremendous outpouring of emotion from baseball fans in 1994. Comments like, "I'll never go to another baseball game again." And similar sentiments from the columnists, both during and after the strike.

Q: How did you feel about Michael Jordan's efforts to become a major league baseball player?

McCarver: I think it was a sincere effort. Ultimately, what it pointed out was how difficult it is for an athlete, even an athlete of Michael's ability and stature, to make the transition to baseball from another sport. And I think Michael's height might have worked against him. I never saw him play, but I've heard he was horrible on any kind of breaking ball. I can understand that. Imagine a man of his height trying to hit a ball that's breaking down.

Q: Tough question coming up. You played for years with Bob Gibson, and you played for years with Steve Carlton. Seventh game of the World Series. Which one would you want pitching for you?

McCarver: I think Steve Carlton would say Bob Gibson; and I think Bob Gibson would say Bob Gibson. So I'll say Bob Gibson. I'd choose Bob—more than any other pitcher I've ever seen—because of his tenacity, his focus, his sense of purpose, and his dramatic leadership qualities. But the Dodgers who played with Sandy Koufax might have a different view.

Q: What about today's pitchers?

McCarver: That's a very difficult question, but I think Roger Clemens would be the guy. Clemens, slightly over Randy Johnson; followed by Greg Maddux and Kevin Brown.

Q: Seventh game of the World Series, bases loaded, bottom of the ninth, you're down by two runs. Who do you want at bat?

McCarver: Willie Mays. I never saw a baseball player who could pick up a team and carry it on his shoulders the way Mays could. If you needed a big hit, nobody was more capable of delivering it than Willie Mays.

Q: What's the best baseball team you ever saw?

McCarver: The 1998 New York Yankees. They could very well be the best baseball team ever. I find it strange that, when people compare teams from different eras, they don't include the pitchers. The 1927 Yankees had several formidable pitchers, but you don't hear much about them. You certainly don't think about pitchers when you think about the 1975 and 1976 Cincinnati Reds. The 1961 Yankees were a great ball club, but people rarely talk about their pitching. When you talk about the 1998 Yankees, you can't help but include the pitchers. My measure of a team's greatness is the number of ways it can beat you. That to me is why the 1998 Yankees are the greatest team I've ever seen. They could win the 1 to 0 game as handily as the 10 to 9 game. If their pitching failed, their hitting carried them along. If their hitting failed, their pitching picked them up. They weren't a great base-stealing team, but they were a great base-running team. And it was all presided over by Joe Torre, who has become one of the great managers of our time.

Q: How do you feel about the idea of the Yankees moving out of Yankee Stadium and possibly even out of the Bronx?

McCarver: I can't picture the New York Yankees in another stadium. I can picture the San Francisco Giants any place but Candlestick Park. I can picture the New York Mets building a new stadium and using Shea as a parking lot. But I cannot picture the Yankees, the most heralded franchise in the world of sports, moving out of Yankee Stadium. Something must be done—and I think it will be done—to renovate the stadium and the surrounding area.

Q: What should baseball do to address the current situation, where some teams spend more and more money to get the best free agents and other teams can no longer afford to be competitive?

McCarver: Marvin Miller once said that, in order to increase competitive balance, you should increase revenue sharing among the teams. I agree with that. It's necessary to a healthy business environment. Also, I have to say, I think Marvin Miller belongs in the Hall of Fame. There's no doubt about it. But so much resentment toward him has built up over the years that there's no real chance of it happening unless it's posthumous.

Q: Should Pete Rose be in the Hall of Fame?

McCarver: That's a difficult question. It would be very awkward for Pete to be in the Hall of Fame until he's reinstated by Major League Baseball. So here we are in a society that's very forgiving, but the powers-that-be have yet to forgive Pete Rose.

Q: If the powers-that-be asked you for a recommendation, what would you say?

McCarver: I'd say it's time; that Pete has been punished enough.

Q: How do you feel about interleague play?

McCarver: I love it. I think it's one of the smartest, most progressive, innovative moves by baseball in years.

Q: What about designated hitters?

McCarver: I hate the DH; always have, and always will. Baseball is a game of strategy, and the DH changes the strategy of the game. I know that some fans prefer 9 to 8 games, as opposed to 3 to 2 games. But real baseball fans—and I'm not just talking about purists—prefer games that include strategy.

Q: Would you like to see baseball adopt some form of instant replay?

McCarver: No. There isn't the need for it that you have in other sports. The main decisions that umpires make are behind home plate, calling balls and strikes, and no one wants automatic robot umpires. Also, it's amazing from a percentage standpoint just how right most umpires' calls are; particularly on plays at first base. Having said that, I do think there's a real problem in baseball today with some umpires not calling the high strike. Umpires should abide by the rulebook. If a pitcher throws a fastball down the heart of the plate just below the letters, call it a strike. I detest it when individual umpires have their own strike zone. A strike is a strike is a strike.

Q: How do you feel about the increasing vocalization of religion in sports?

McCarver: I think that religion and your belief in God should be between you and The Maker. You don't take batting practice in church, and you shouldn't bring church into the clubhouse. Also, to say that everything that happens in a baseball game is God's will, that it was God's will for you to throw a fat fastball that the other guy hit out of the ballpark; that, to me, is a ludicrous approach to sports.

Q: What did Mark McGwire and Sammy Sosa do for baseball last year?

McCarver: I'm not one who thinks that baseball came back because of 1998. I think baseball was back after the Yankees won the World Series in 1996. But 1998 wrapped it all up very nicely, and McGwire and Sosa were the two main individual stories out of many stories that made the 1998 season great. You had Kerry Wood striking out twenty batters in his fifth major league start; David Wells's perfect game; Ricky Henderson leading the league in stolen bases at age thirty-nine; Barry Bonds hitting his four hundredth home run to go with four hundred stolen bases. But Mark's accomplishment was extraordinary, and Sammy's was too. The remarkable sportsmanship and grace they showed toward one another and toward the fans rubbed off on the entire nation. Who can ever forget Mark McGwire hitting his sixty-second home run and going into the stands to hug Roger Maris's family? That was better than any movie. You can't write things like that.

Q: How would you compare McGwire with Babe Ruth?

McCarver: Babe Ruth was the best baseball player ever. Not too many knowledgeable people would argue with that. But from a power stand-point, what Mark McGwire accomplished last year entitles him to be mentioned in the same breath as Babe Ruth. He might have made it seem effortless. But everybody knows that one of the most difficult things in the world to do is to hit a baseball thrown by a pitcher in an unpredictable location, and have the strength, timing, and hand-eye coordination to lift it up and out of the ballpark. Mark McGwire did that seventy times last year. That's extraordinary.

Air travel is essential to modern sports. But with professional athletes log-
ging millions of miles in the air each year, one has to wonder what would
happen if disaster struck. In the early 1990s, The National (a daily sports
newspaper) asked me to find out.

If Disaster Strikes

As a young man, Muhammad Ali was terrified of flying. He talked of withdrawing from the 1960 Olympics because the United States Olympic Committee wouldn't let him take a boat to Rome. Early in his professional career, rather than fly, he traveled in a red-and-white bus with the name "Cassius Clay" painted on the side. "One good thing about busses," he proclaimed, "is when they break down, they don't fall thirty thousand feet." Finally, Ali got used to flying, but that didn't keep him from being outpointed on a shuttle flight from Washington D.C. to New York. As the plane was readying for takeoff, a stewardess instructed him to fasten his seatbelt.

"Superman don't need no seatbelt," the champ responded.

"Mr. Ali," the stewardess said sweetly, "Superman don't need no plane."

Former football coach and current television color commentator John Madden is cut from the Ali mold. For years, Madden has suffered from a well-publicized fear of flying. He still travels from game to game in a forty-foot, $480,000 customized bus, equipped with a bed, shower, pantry, telephones, and VCR. Madden says the bus enables him to see America the way it should be seen. It also keeps him firmly on the ground.

Ali and Madden are hardly unique. Millions of people fear flying. Airplane accidents have taken the lives of Roberto Clemente, Rocky Marciano, and many other celebrated athletes. Even amid the recently heightened concerns about a terrorist action aimed at a sporting event, the greatest fear of America's sports establishment—given the enormous number of hours athletes now spend on airplanes—is that an entire team will be lost in an air disaster.

The images are there. A plane carrying the old Minneapolis Lakers developed mechanical problems and was forced to make an emergency landing in a Midwestern cornfield. Recently, a small aircraft strayed perilously close to a flight carrying the Oakland Athletics.

In the world of amateur sports, the unthinkable has already occurred.

★ In 1961, a Belgian airliner carrying the seventeen-member U.S. figure-skating team to the world championships in Prague crashed in Brussels. There were no survivors. An entire generation of America's finest skaters perished.

★ In 1970, forty-three members of the Marshall University football team were among seventy-five dead when a Southern Airways DC-9 crashed in the mountains near Huntington, West Virginia.

★ In 1977, all fourteen players on the University of Evansville basketball team died when their chartered DC-3 crashed just after takeoff in Evansville, Indiana. The Purple Aces had won five national small-college championships.

★ In 1980, fourteen boxers and eight team officials representing the United States Amateur Athletic Union were killed in the crash of a Polish jet in Warsaw. Among the dead was Tom (Sarge) Johnson, who in 1976 had guided the United States Olympic Boxing Team to five gold medals in Montreal.

These tragedies generated enormous grief. But if a professional team is ever wiped out, there will be extraordinary financial consequences as well. Thus, each of America's major sports leagues has a disaster plan to cover possibilities such as an airplane crash or the collapse of an arena roof while a game is in progress. It's not a topic that the rulers of sport like to think about, let alone discuss in public. But recently, officials of each league shared details of their disaster plans with *The National*.

None of the plans deal with every contingency. For example, they speak of "accidents," leaving open the question of what happens if a team is decimated by illness or a crazed assassin bombs a locker room. Likewise, they fail to specify what will occur if two separate accidents take a toll that would trigger a disaster plan if it were a single incident

To deal with these gaps, the NFL gives its commissioner the authority to adjust disaster procedures subject to approval by the club owners. To the extent that Major League Baseball's disaster plans offer leeway, the league presidents hold that power. The same holds true for the NBA and NHL, whose chief executive officers are accorded a right of interpretation subject to approval by their respective boards of governors.

One can only hope that these league disaster plans will remain obscure footnotes to history. But if needed, the planning summarized in the following pages is there.

The National Football League

Under the current NFL disaster plan, a disaster is deemed to have occurred when a team loses fifteen or more players in an accident. A "lost" player is one who has been killed or incapacitated for the remainder of the season. If a team suffers a disaster, the commissioner is empowered to determine whether it should play or cancel its remaining games. Should its season be canceled, the team will have first choice in the next college draft and will be allocated players at no cost from the other teams in a special draft. In that draft, each of the other teams may protect thirty-four players from its active and reserve lists combined. The damaged team may select one player from each club until it has replaced the exact number of players lost. The process extends to a second round if the numbers warrant.

Should the commissioner order that the "disaster team" continue its season, there would be no special draft, but a number of allowances would be made, including priority on all waiver claims and a special procedure for replacing quarterbacks if a team is left with fewer than two. Other teams may protect two quarterbacks, and any quarterback selected by this process would be returned to his original team at the end of the season.

The NFL also provides that the commissioner can declare a "near disaster" if a team loses more than one but fewer that fifteen players. Here, the skill of the players lost is relevant. If for instance, a team lost eight starters, the "near disaster" plan might be activated. "Near disaster" benefits would be the same as if the club had suffered a disaster and its season was continued.

Major League Baseball

Major League Baseball regards team disasters as a league problem rather than a matter to be dealt with by the commissioner's office. In fact, the American and National Leagues have different disaster plans, both of which date to the 1960s.

The American League plan is triggered if six or more active players from any one team are killed or injured seriously enough in an accident to miss thirty consecutive games. In that event, the other AL teams would each submit a list of four players—one pitcher, one catcher, one infielder, and one outfielder—who were active before the preceding August 31. The disabled club would then choose the number of players lost, minus five. No more than one player could be drafted from each of the other teams until one player had been drafted from each of them. League rules require that a team replace lost players with others playing the same position. A team that lost six pitchers, for instance, could not use the disaster draft as an opportunity to acquire a designated hitter.

The National League plan is triggered if seven or more active players from any one team are killed or disabled in an accident. Unlike the American League, the National League leaves it up to the league president to define "disabled" on a case-by-case basis. The rules suggest a time frame of sixty calendar days of lost service.

Under the National League plan, each team other than the disabled club must submit a list of twelve active players available to be drafted. Specific requirements regarding the listed players, such as the date and duration of their active status, depend upon the date of the disaster. The disabled club must choose the number of players lost, minus six. No more than one player can be drafted from each of the other teams until one player has been drafted from each of them.

In both leagues, the disabled club assumes all responsibility for a drafted player's physical condition, and receives his contract outright. In return, it must pay each club from which a player is chosen—$100,000 in the American League, $175,000 in the National League—amounts covered by the league's insurance policy.

The National Basketball Association

The NBA disaster plan is triggered when a team loses five or more players to death or permanent disability. In such event, the league would hold a "disaster draft." Each of the other teams would be allowed to freeze five players from its twelve-man roster. The disabled club would then choose the number of players it lost, but no more than one from each team.

The NBA's rules, more than those of the other leagues, offer the possibility of a team improving itself through a disaster and the succeeding draft. Unlike the NFL, the NBA treats all lost players the same in terms of value. Also, the full complement of players lost can be replaced. Thus, an NBA team that loses its starting five wouldn't be made whole by the disaster draft. But a team that lost its eight through twelfth players could gain by replacing them with five "sixth men" from other teams. The NBA has an insurance policy to compensate both the disabled club and teams that lose players in the draft, but it prefers not to make details of the policy public.

The National Hockey League

The NHL's "Emergency Rehabilitation Plan" is complicated by the fact that NHL teams don't have set rosters like teams in the other major sports. NHL clubs dress eighteen regular players and two goalies for each game. But they practice and often travel with additional "active" players who are interchangeable with the first twenty. Still, the league has a formula to deal with disasters.

If an NHL club suffers an accident resulting in the death or permanent disability of five or more active players, the league president must convene a meeting of the board of governors to seek effective rehabilitation. The board would assess the loss and replace the players through the voluntary sale of player contracts to the disaster club. After that sale, if the damaged club still had fewer than fourteen regular players and one goalie, a draft would commence until those levels were achieved (and could continue, at the damaged club's option, until eighteen regulars and two goalies were on its roster). In the draft, each team could protect ten regular players and one goalie. Also, all first-year NHL players and players under age twenty would be exempt. No more than one player could be chosen from each team in the draft. Clubs that lost players in the draft would be compensated by insurance.

Author's Note: These plans have changed in recent years. Let's hope there's never a need to implement any of them.

The NFL has changed its overtime rule since this article was written in 2003. The rule is still a work in progress, but it's getting better.

The NFL Overtime Rule

The first overtime game in National Football League history was a 1955 preseason contest between the New York Giants and Los Angeles Rams. The game was played in Portland, Oregon. Its promoter, Harry Glickman, had asked the league for permission to play a sudden-death overtime should the occasion arise. The Giants and Rams were tied 17–17 at the end of regulation play. Three minutes and twenty-eight seconds later, the Rams won on a two-yard run by Tank Younger.

The first NFL overtime that mattered came in the historic 1958 championship game between the Giants and Baltimore Colts. There have been seventeen postseason overtime games since then.

Where regular-season play is concerned, the National Football League enacted a rule in 1974 that calls for one period of sudden-death play if a game is tied at the end of four quarters. That rule is well intentioned. After all, as Ara Parsegian once opined, "A tie is like kissing your sister." But the NFL has a problem. Too often, in overtime contests, the biggest play of the day is the coin flip to determine which team has the first possession in overtime.

Since 1974, the team that has won the coin toss has won 52 percent of all overtime games and lost 43 percent. Five percent of overtime contests have ended in ties. That puts a significant premium on winning a coin toss. Moreover, 28 percent of overtime games have ended on the first possession.

It gets worse. In 1994, the NFL moved the starting point for kickoffs from the 35 to the thirty yard line, which means that receiving teams get better field position now than in the past. Also, over the years, field-goal kickers have become more accurate. Thus, since 1994, the percentage of teams winning on the first overtime possession has risen to 33 percent. Last year, teams that had the ball first won 40 percent of NFL overtime games on their first possession.

Not everyone is troubled by these numbers. "I like defense," declares Giants co-owner Wellington Mara. "If you can't stop a team when it gets the ball, you don't deserve to win."

But Gene Upshaw (president of the NFL Players Association) says, "If you get into overtime, you should have a fair chance to win."

And no matter how one views the situation, the outcome of a game shouldn't rest on whether a 320-pound defensive tackle says "heads" or "tails."

Moreover, the pro rule is in stark contrast to college overtime, which has fans on their feet cheering for every play. The NCAA adopted an overtime format in 1996, under which each team gets the ball on its opponent's twenty-five yard line and keeps possession until it scores, loses the ball, or gives it up on downs. The college system reached its zenith in the January 2003 national championship game when Ohio State beat Miami 31–24 in double overtime.

The NFL regards the college overtime rule as anathema. It says it will never adopt an overtime system that sets up an endless number of possessions, bloats the score, and devalues years of NFL records to determine a winner. It also notes that, with sudden-death overtime, there's drama in knowing that a game can end on any play. And when it ends, it ends on a score; not an incomplete pass.

Still, as NFL commissioner Paul Tagliabue acknowledges, "The advantage of receiving first in overtime is becoming unbalanced." Tagliabue predicted in November 2002 that team owners would scrap the sudden-death format at their annual meeting in March 2003. He anticipated a new overtime rule that called for each team to get at least one possession. Then, if the game were still tied after each team had the ball once, the sudden-death rule would apply. In other words, receiving first would give a team an advantage in sudden death but only after being at a disadvantage for the first two possessions. Twenty-four votes were needed for passage of the proposal. Only seventeen teams voted for it.

Thus, in August 2003, Tagliabue floated another proposal. This one called for overtime to become, in effect, a fifth quarter. Whichever team had the ball at the end of regulation time would simply keep possession at the same yard-line.

"You don't need to kick off to start the overtime," Tagliabue reasoned. "The big problem is the randomness of the coin toss to start the period. So you reward the teams by whatever position they've earned through four quarters. If you're on the eighteen-yard line when the game ends, you get that position in overtime. It takes out the random element, the coin toss, which drives coaches crazy. It lets the offenses and defenses continue to play without inserting that one random event."

But as CBS Sports president Sean McManus noted, Tagliabue's proposal would diminish the final two minutes of regulation play. "That's the best programming on television," said McManus. "I wouldn't do anything to mess with the last two minutes of regulation of an NFL game. You can change the overtime; but please, don't think about changing those two minutes."

Meanwhile, here's one vote for a simple solution. Even though the name of the game is FOOTball, there's something inherently unsatisfying about an overtime game ending on a field goal. And 72 percent of all NFL overtime games that have ended on the first possession did just that.

Keep sudden-death overtime the way it is with one significant exception. Require a touchdown or a safety, not a field goal, to win.

I've followed Columbia football as a long-suffering fan for decades.

Roar, Lion, Roar: Columbia Football

The first two college football games ever played were between Princeton and Rutgers in 1869. The third college gridiron match-up was between Columbia and Rutgers a year later. Columbia lost that game and has been losing ever since.

How bad is Columbia Lions football?

Drumroll, please . . .

★ Entering the 2003 season, Columbia had lost 559 games. Only four teams in college football history (Northwestern, Kansas State, Richmond, and VMI) have lost more.

★ Columbia's overall winning percentage is .388. Only Austin Peay and Siena sport a more dismal number.

★ The last Columbia coach to compile a winning record was Charles Crowley, who relinquished the reins in 1929.

★ During an unlucky thirteen-year period between 1979 and 1991, Columbia had 10 wins, 116 losses, and 2 ties.

★ Columbia has had two winning seasons in the past thirty-one years.

In other words, failure is a gridiron tradition at Columbia. Still, there have been moments of glory.

★ In 1915, after football had been banned for nine years, Columbia returned to the playing field and was undefeated in five games.

★ Lou Little coached the Lions for twenty-seven campaigns (1930– 1956), including a four-year stretch from 1931 to 1934 when Columbia went 29-4-2, culminating in a 7–0 victory over Stanford in the 1934 Rose Bowl.

★ In 1938, after trailing 18–6 at halftime, Sid Luckman quarterbacked the Lions to a historic upset over mighty Army at West Point.

* In 1947, at Baker Field, Columbia recovered from a 20–7 halftime deficit to upset Army again, beating a cadet team that hadn't lost in thirty-two games by a score of 21–20.

In 1956, Columbia joined Harvard, Yale, Princeton, Pennsylvania, Cornell, Dartmouth, and Brown to form the Ivy League. The league's signature requirement is that each member institution engage in intercollegiate competition in accordance with rules that place academic priorities over athletics.

Columbia tied Harvard for the Ivy League title in 1961, but high points since then have been few and far between. The low point is known simply as "The Streak." Starting with a 31–6 loss to Cornell in 1983, the Lions lost forty-four games in a row. The Streak ended with a 16–13 triumph over Princeton in the fourth game of the 1988 campaign.

Still, despite this record of futility, eight former Lions have played in the NFL since the formation of the Ivy League. The most successful of these was George Starke, who anchored the offensive line for the Washington Redskins from 1973 through 1984 and was "Head Hog" during Washington's 1983 Super Bowl win over Miami. Then there's Marcellus Wiley, who played defensive end for the Buffalo Bills from 1997 to 2000 and has been with the San Diego Chargers ever since.

Three Columbia quarterbacks of Ivy vintage followed in the footsteps of Sid Luckman to play in the NFL. Marty Domres was chosen by San Diego with the ninth overall pick in the 1969 draft. Three years later, he replaced the fabled Johnny Unitas as starting quarterback for the Baltimore Colts. Archie Roberts was drafted by the Cleveland Browns, opted for medical school, and wound up calling signals for the Miami Dolphins. John Witkowski quarterbacked the Detroit Lions.

Wide receiver Bruce Stephens and running back John Chirico each had a cup of coffee with the New York Jets. Tight end Jerry Zawadzkas played briefly for Detroit.

At this point in the narrative, I should confess that I'm a recovering Columbia football junkie. I attended college and law school at Columbia for seven years that encompassed the 1963 through 1969 campaigns. During those years, the only home game I missed fell on the same day that the Law School Aptitude Test was administered.

The first Columbia game I saw was the home opener against Princeton in September 1963. It was Homecoming Weekend; hopes were high; and Columbia boosters actually rented a lion that they placed in a cage behind the north end zone. Contrary to expectations, the lion did not roar. Instead, it fell asleep and slept for most of the game. So did the Columbia offense. Princeton won 7–6.

That was a harbinger of things to come. During my seven years on campus, Columbia's record was 15-46-2. During one particularly frustrating season, the starting quarterback was so limited that he had to pitch out to the fullback every time the Lions wanted to throw a long pass.

After graduation, I remained loyal, attending several games a year. I remember coming home late one afternoon after sitting in freezing temperatures whipped by a biting wind, having watched Columbia lose to Holy Cross. If memory serves me correctly, the score was 77–28, which is a bad way to lose a football game. I was cold and cranky. A friend asked, "Why do you subject yourself to that?"

Now I limit myself to one game a year. This year, it was Columbia versus Bucknell.

Columbia has a new head football coach. He's thirty-six-year-old Bob Shoop; a former assistant at Boston College, who took over the reins after Columbia went 1 and 9 and was winless in the Ivy League last year.

The game was slated for 7:00 PM at Baker Field, which is located in a surprisingly bucolic setting at the northern tip of Manhattan. It was a classic early-autumn evening; on the balmy side with a gentle breeze coming from the Hudson River.

Columbia had lost its season opener to Fordham 37–30 to extend its losing streak to ten games. Bucknell came into the contest with two wins and one defeat.

After a scoreless first quarter, Columbia took the lead on a one-yard run by Ayo Oluwole. A low snap led to a blocked extra point. Four minutes later, after recovering a Bucknell fumble, the Lions scored again on a thirty-one-yard pass from Jeff Otis to Wade Fletcher. Again, the extra point was blocked.

12–0 Lions.

One might have expected joy at this point, but the crowd was pretty quiet. Columbia fans haven't had much to cheer about over the years, so they're out of practice. Also, Columbia with a lead is a bit like Charlie Brown getting ready to kick a football with Lucy holding. There's an uncomfortable feeling that something bad is about to happen. Those two blocked extra points stood out like a sore thumb.

Bucknell scored six points on two field goals to narrow the margin to 12–6 at the half. Then, with 3:58 remaining in the third quarter, the Bison grabbed the lead on a twelve-yard run by quarterback Antwan Kennedy and a properly executed extra point. Another field goal made it 16–12 Bucknell.

That's how things stood when Columbia took possession of the ball on its own twenty-seven-yard line with 3:27 left to play. Surprisingly, the Lions marched downfield . . . First down . . . First down . . . First down . . .

But the clock was ticking . . . First and ten on the Bucknell twenty-eight . . . First and goal on the Bucknell nine with thirty-three seconds left to play.

Now the crowd was on its feet . . . Roaring . . . There was a four-yard gain . . . Twenty-one seconds left; ball on the Bucknell five . . . Jeff Otis dropped back to pass and fired a strike to Travis Chmelka, who dove for the ball in the back of the end zone and somehow managed to keep a foot inbounds . . .

TOUCHDOWN ! ! ! Lions win 19–16. The first victory of the Bob Shoop era.

It was exciting. And one week later, Columbia did it again, beating Princeton 33–27 on a forty-nine-yard "Hail Mary" pass from Otis to Wade Fletcher on the last play of the game.

So listen up, sports fans. There's something very nice about Ivy League football. Students can walk in at the last minute and get good tickets for a game. They don't have to stand on line for hours to sit in a far-away section behind one of the end zones.

Also, and far more important, Columbia football players are real students. They live in dormitories with their contemporaries. They take the same classes as other students. They get, in every sense of the word, a college EDUCATION.

And I should add that "Roar Lion Roar" is one of the great fight songs in the nation.

Someday, the lion that is Columbia football will roar again.

This was a companion piece to my article about Columbia football.

Columbia Basketball

Last Sunday, the National Football League playoffs were building in drama. The Indianapolis Colts were challenging the Kansas City Chiefs, and the Green Bay Packers were testing the Philadelphia Eagles.

So naturally, I was at home watching football on television. Right?

Wrong! Actually, I was at Levien Gym on the Columbia University campus, watching a basketball game between my alma mater and Farleigh-Dickinson.

Columbia's basketball history began in 1900 and, by late 1903, the Lions were a powerhouse. Throw out the rebuilding season of 1907–08, and Columbia compiled an intercollegiate record of ninety-nine wins against ten losses in the nine campaigns that ended in 1912.

The next half-century saw some good Columbia basketball teams and also some bad ones. The best stretch of sustained excellence came from the 1947–48 season through the 1956–57 campaign, when the Lions won 165 games and lost 68. Three players of note stood out during that time.

Jack Molinas was a mainstay of the team that went undefeated during the 1950–51 regular season. Two years later, he was the Lions' captain. Molinas was a prolific scorer and still holds the Columbia record for most rebounds in a single game. Of more dubious note, he began fixing games while in college, continued to do so as an NBA player, and was permanently barred from the league by NBA president Maurice Podoloff. Thereafter, Molinas continued his unsavory ways and ultimately received a fifteen-year prison sentence for conspiracy to fix twenty-five games involving twenty-two players at twelve colleges. After being paroled, he moved to California, where he engaged in a variety of business ventures ranging from the production of adult films to stock fraud. He was executed gangland-style in 1975.

Franklin Thomas, one of the Ivy League's first black stars, is still Columbia's career leader in rebounds. A three-time letterman and captain of the 1955–56 Lions team, he's best known to the public at large for having been president of the Ford Foundation from 1979 through 1996. Prior to that, Thomas served as president of the Bedford Stuyvesant Restoration Corporation, deputy police commissioner for the New York City Police Department, and an assistant U.S. attorney for the United States Department of Justice.

Chet Forte, the 1956–57 Lions captain, edged out Wilt Chamberlain in balloting for the United Press International "Player of the Year" award in his senior season. Despite being only 5 feet, 8 inches tall, Forte set a Columbia record for most points in a season. His career scoring average of 24.8 points per game is still the Lions standard. Forte later became one of the most celebrated men in sports media as the director of ABC's *Monday Night Football*. But like Molinas, he had a gambling problem. He was a compulsive gambler and, in 1990, plead guilty to charges of mail fraud, wire fraud, and income tax evasion; acts committed as part of an effort to support his gambling habit.

By the time I enrolled at Columbia in September 1963, the Lions' basketball fortunes were in decline. Home games were played in anti-quated University Hall; a classic structure replete with architectural columns that blocked the view of fans and looked as though they'd been built during the Age of Pericles. Columbia had suffered through six straight losing seasons. Two more would follow.

During the 1965–66 campaign, I started doing play-by-play of Columbia basketball games for WKCR (the student-run radio station). That same season, the Lions' fortunes turned. Led by seven-foot Dave Newmark, the team posted an 18-6 record. The future looked bright. Then Newmark put his hand through a window in a freak dormitory accident and missed the entire 1966–67 season. Without him, the team went 11 and 14.

Still, hopes were high. Freshmen were ineligible for varsity play in those years. But Columbia's freshman team was led by Jim McMillian and Heyward Dotson; two of the best players ever to wear a Lions uniform. Three glorious seasons followed.

Newmark was back for the 1967–68 campaign; McMillian was the greatest player in Columbia basketball history; and Dotson was superb. After three early-season losses, the Lions caught fire at the Holiday Festival at Madison Square Garden. In three nights, Columbia beat West Virginia,

Louisville (the #2 team in the nation), and St. John's. Thus began a sixteen-game winning streak that led to the Ivy League title and an appearance in what is now known as the "Sweet Sixteen" of the NCAA postseason tournament. At one point, the Lions were ranked fourth in the nation. It's hard to imagine that an Ivy League team will ever be ranked that high again.

The season ended on a two-point NCAA-tournament overtime loss to Davidson. But with all five starters returning, Columbia's future looked bright.

Then the future got darker. Newmark opted for the pros with a year of college eligibility remaining. Penn and Princeton turned into basketball powerhouses. Columbia went 20-4 in 1968-69, beating Stanford, Purdue, and Georgetown, but finished second in the Ivy League at a time when only one team from each league was invited to the NCAA tournament and league rules prohibited NIT play. In 1969–70, the Lions posted a 20-5 record with victories over Penn State, Wake Forest, and Villanova, but again finished second in Ivy competition.

McMillian, a three-time All-American, would go on to play nine seasons in the NBA. His best year as a pro was the 1971–72 campaign, when he averaged 18.8 points a game for the Los Angeles Lakers. But that number hardly tells the full story. On November 4, 1971, troubled by chronic knee problems, Laker great Elgin Baylor announced his retirement. The following night, McMillian took his place in the starting line-up, scored 22 points, and pulled down 13 rebounds. The Lakers went on to win 33 games in a row (the longest winning streak in the history of professional sports) and capped the season with their first NBA championship in Los Angeles. McMillian's teammates included Wilt Chamberlain, Jerry West, Gail Goodrich, Keith Erickson, and Pat Riley.

McMillian's departure from Columbia was followed by a series of losing campaigns. There was a brief renaissance in the mid-1970s, but the Lions have had only one winning season in the past twenty-four years. Last season, Columbia won only two games against twenty-five losses and went winless for the first time ever in Ivy League play. Entering the 2003–2004 campaign, the Lions had played 2,144 intercollegiate basketball games, winning 1077 and losing 1,067. There is now danger that Columbia's all-time record will slip below the .500 mark for the first time since 1903.

As a once-rabid Columbia basketball fan, I still go to a game each year. This time, I wanted to see the Lions win. Columbia versus Farleigh-Dickinson seemed like a good choice.

The opponent, to be more specific, was Farleigh-Dickinson at Florham-Madison. The Devils, as this FD squad is known, should be distinguished from the Farleigh-Dickinson Knights, whose campus is in Teaneck. The Knights compete in the Northeast Conference and play pretty good basketball. The Devils are less talented. Their record entering the Columbia game was five wins and five losses. That was superior to the Lions' three victories against nine defeats. But a closer look revealed that Farleigh-Dickinson's wins had come against Manhattanville, Wesleyan, Stevens, Hunter, and New York Tech, while they had lost to John Jay, Delaware Valley, Staten Island, William Paterson, and Gwynedd Mercy.

It was the first meeting ever between the two teams. Fans filtered into the gym throughout the game, but there were only 138 spectators on hand for the opening tip. That led to the suggestion that, instead of the public-address announcer introducing the starting line-ups, the players should go into the stands and shake hands with everyone. Ultimately, pregame festivities were conducted in the usual way.

Columbia took an early 15–8 lead and was ahead 38–25 at the half. The last twenty minutes of play were more of the same, with the Lions winning 77–45. The most promising aspect of the game was the fact that Columbia is a young team. Only two of its sixteen players (and one starter) are seniors. The Lions' best hoopsters are 6 feet, 5 inch junior Matt Preston, 6-9 sophomore Dodson Worthington, and 6-8 sophomore Dragutin Kravic. That bodes well for the future. If first-year coach Joe Jones can entice a solid class of recruits to Morningside Heights later this year, good things might happen for Columbia basketball.

And to complete the Columbia trilogy . . .

Columbia Baseball

Moments of athletic glory for Columbia have been few and far between. The university is known for struggling in major sports. Its sole Ivy League titles in football (1961) and basketball (1968) are distant memories. College baseball might not be "major," but the Lions have struggled there too.

It wasn't always so. All one has to do is go back 102 years to September 1903, when sixteen-year-old Eddie Collins enrolled at Columbia. Collins starred at quarterback and became captain of the Lions' baseball team. He was talented enough that, during the summer after his junior year of college, he played for the Philadelphia Athletics, using the name "Sullivan" to maintain his college eligibility. Unfortunately, he was found out and ruled ineligible for further intercollegiate play. So during his senior year at Columbia, he coached the Lions in baseball before returning to the major leagues.

Collins played twenty-five seasons for the Athletics and Chicago White Sox. His Hall of Fame credentials included 3,315 base hits and a .333 lifetime batting average. He also stole 743 bases, making him one of five players in major league history with at least 3,000 hits and 500 stolen bases.

The other jewel in Columbia baseball lore is Lou Gehrig. "The Iron Horse" spent two years at Columbia. In some respects, they were unhappy ones. Gehrig came from a poor background and felt that many of his classmates looked down on him. In autumn 1922, he played halfback and defensive lineman for a Lions football team that compiled a 5 and 4 record. His greatness, of course, was on the baseball diamond.

Gehrig played one season (1923) consisting of nineteen games for Columbia. He was primarily a first baseman and pitcher, although he saw action once in right field. His statistics at the plate were impressive: twenty-eight base hits in sixty-three at bats for a .444 batting average;

seven doubles, two triples, and seven home runs for a .937 slugging percentage; and twenty-four runs scored. On the mound, he won six games and lost four with one no decision. In five of his eleven outings he struck out ten or more men.

On April 18, 1923, the day that Yankee Stadium opened, Gehrig took the mound for Columbia against Williams and struck out seventeen batters; a Lions record that still stands. At the end of the season, he signed to play professional baseball.

In seventeen years with the New York Yankees, Gehrig compiled a .340 lifetime batting average and hit 493 home runs. He ranks third among all major leaguers in career RBIs, third in slugging percentage, and eighth in runs scored. Prior to being robbed of his skills by ALS, he played in 2,130 consecutive major league games.

Gehrig and Collins were voted into the Baseball Hall of Fame in 1939. To this day, Columbia is the only college with two inductees in Cooperstown. The dual enshrinement is particularly remarkable given the fact that, in the early decades of the twentieth century, only a handful of quality major league players went to college. Christy Mathewson graduated from Bucknell. Frankie Frisch (Fordham), George Sisler (Michigan), and Paul Waner (Oklahoma State) also earned degrees. But they were the exception rather than the rule.

After Gehrig, baseball glory at Columbia was rare. On May 17, 1939, the Lions made sports history when a home game against Princeton became the first televised sporting event ever. At the time, fewer than four hundred sets were owned by the general public. The contest was televised by W2XBS, an experimental station owned by NBC. Princeton won 2 to 1 in ten innings.

Die-hard Columbia fans note that Sandy Koufax studied at the university's School of General Studies in the 1950s. But Koufax never played ball for the Lions. The most recent alumnus to make an impact in the big leagues after taking the field for Columbia was Gene Larkin (class of 1984). On October 27, 1991, Larkin stepped to the plate with the bases loaded in the bottom of the tenth inning of a scoreless tie between the Minnesota Twins and Atlanta Braves in the seventh game of the World Series and singled to left field, bringing a world championship to Minnesota.

That brings us to the present. Columbia's 2005 baseball season consists of forty-six games scheduled on twenty-eight dates between March 5 and May 1. In Gehrig's day, baseball and football were played on South Field, located in the middle of the campus at 116th Street between Broadway and Amsterdam Avenue. Now home games are contested at the Baker Field Sports Complex at the northern tip of Manhattan.

This past Sunday afternoon (April 17, 2005), the Lions played a doubleheader against Cornell. The first game was scheduled to start at noon, but was pushed back to 12:30 so prospective fans could watch the end of a women's lacrosse match between the schools on an adjacent field.

The Cornell women won 15 to 5. Then the crowd, such as it was, gathered at the baseball diamond on benches carved into a hill behind home plate. The benches are fashioned from unfinished wood similar to that used for railroad ties and are separated from the playing field by a high chain-link backstop.

These are hard times for Columbia baseball. The team entered Sunday's doubleheader with a twelve-game losing streak and a 2005 record of 3 wins against 26 losses. Its pitching staff had given up 8.72 runs per game and surrendered ten or more runs on twelve occasions. The Lions' lone Ivy League victory came on a 4–2 triumph over Penn. Its other two wins were against Farleigh-Dickinson and Vermont.

Cornell was 9 and 14 with two of those wins coming against Columbia.

It was a perfect spring day with the temperature in the low-seventies and a gentle breeze coming in from the Hudson River. The sky was a clear Columbia blue. Pursuant to NCAA rules governing doubleheaders, each game was slated for seven innings. Forty-seven spectators (all of whom were admitted free) were in the stands when a recording of the National Anthem was played.

Cornell drew first blood. The Columbia pitcher was John Bauman, a 6 feet, 7 inch freshman making his third start. The third Cornell batter whacked a fastball over the fence in straight-away left field, and the Big Red led 1–0.

The Lions came back in the bottom of the first, scoring two runs on a walk, an error, a wild pitch, another walk, and a single. They added another run in the third inning on a single, a wild pitch, a stolen base, and a throwing error by the Cornell catcher. Then, in the fourth inning, the roof caved in . . . for Cornell.

A hit batter and walk followed by a single to right put the Lions ahead 4 to 1.

Tighe Holden, Columbia's 6 feet, 6 inch, 250-pound first baseman strode to the plate with two men on base and one out.

The crowd had grown to 150 people. Lacrosse players had showered and were watching the action. They'd been joined by late arrivals from church and Sunday brunch.

Mighty Tighe swung.

WHACK!

The ball rocketed over the right-field fence, and Columbia led 7 to 1.

Cornell narrowed the margin to 7–3 with two runs in the top of the fifth on a single, a stolen base, two Columbia errors, and a balk. That was enough to make the local faithful nervous; particularly since Bauman's fastball was losing its pop. But the Lions sealed things in the bottom of the sixth inning with three more runs on a single, a triple, and two Cornell errors (Columbia and Cornell make lots of errors).

Daniel Ramos pitched the final inning for the Lions in relief of Bauman and gave up a run on two hits. But it was too little too late for the Big Red. At precisely 2:42 PM, Columbia had its fourth win of the season, a 10–4 triumph. Then the Lions went out and lost to Cornell by the same 10–4 score in the nightcap.

LeRoy Neiman has had a front-row seat on the sports scene for almost fifty years.

I've Been to the Mountaintop: A Sports Fan Is Painted by LeRoy Neiman

Actually, it isn't a painting. He used pastels.

But it's more than a sketch. "A study," he called it.

And with a simple act of kindness, LeRoy Neiman added to the good deeds he has performed over a lifetime.

Neiman was born in Minnesota on June 8, 1921. His father (Charles Runquist) was an unskilled laborer, who abandoned the family when LeRoy was young. His mother remarried twice, and LeRoy took the surname of one of his stepfathers.

As a child, Neiman was drawn to art. In grade school, he put pen-and-ink tattoos on the arms of fellow students. In high school, although lacking in formal training, he created posters for athletic events and earned pocket cash by painting images of meat, fruit, and vegetables on grocery store windows. Later, as a mess sergeant in the army during World War II, he designed posters, painted sexually suggestive murals in mess halls, and otherwise served the Allied cause.

After the war, Neiman studied at the St. Paul Art Center and the Art Institute of Chicago. Then he began work as a fashion illustrator and, while freelancing in Chicago, met a young copywriter named Hugh Hefner.

In 1953, Hefner launched *Playboy*, and Neiman became the magazine's "official" artist. His first noteworthy contribution was the creation of "Femlin"—a tiny character who has appeared on the *Playboy* jokes page in every issue since August 1955. Then, beginning in 1958 and continuing for the next fifteen years, Neiman traveled around the globe for *Playboy* to paint a monthly feature entitled "Man At His Leisure." His artwork celebrated the privileged world of "beautiful people" and gave his audience an intimate look at the most elite places and events on the planet; all from a glorifying point of view.

"When I paint," LeRoy acknowledged, "I consider the public presence of a person; the surface facade. I'm less concerned with how people look when they wake up or how they act at home. A person's public presence reflects his own efforts at image development. I focus on the beauty and the best. Sure, I'd rather paint a Rolls Royce than a Volkswagen."

Meanwhile, Neiman was carefully cultivating his own image to make himself famous and wealthy. As Hugh Hefner later observed, "LeRoy quite intentionally invented himself as a flamboyant artist in much the same way that I became Mr. Playboy." Neiman agrees, saying, "I guess I created LeRoy Neiman. Nobody else told me how to do it."

Neiman was the first artist to successfully tap into the mass media. And over time, the Neiman style with its splashes of intense color and sense of motion became nationally known. In the late 1960s, he appeared regularly on New York Jets football telecasts as the team's "official artist in residence." At the 1972 Munich Olympics, he sketched live for ABC's cameras. Four years later at the Montreal games, he painted a huge mural for a national television audience and entered into a deal with Burger King for the distribution of five Neiman posters in conjunction with an Olympics promotion. Purists groaned, but LeRoy himself later said, "Those posters were distributed to kids who had never seen a painting before in their lives. And the Burger King project exposed my work to millions of people, so it was not a bad thing."

In his most prolific years, Neiman created as many as a thousand pieces annually. "I work fast," he said. "Sometimes I do forty sketches at one event. A painting generally takes me from two to three weeks."

It's a point of pride for LeRoy that no one but the artist himself has ever put a brush to one of his canvases. He has painted everything from nudes backstage at the Lido in Paris to the CD box for Frank Sinatra's recording of "Duets." However, he's best known for his sports scenes and portraits of athletes.

"Concentrating on sports helped me," Neiman admits. "There hasn't been any sports art to speak of, so I've had the field pretty much to myself." And he has made the most of that exclusivity, elevating himself to a special status in the world of sports.

When LeRoy Neiman paints an athlete or an event, it's a stamp of importance. He has been the official artist for five Olympics and crafted images of countless Super Bowls, NBA playoffs, the World Series, the Grand Prix at Monaco, Oxford versus Cambridge on the Thames, horse-racing, cricket, bullfights, tennis, golf, hockey, billiards, yachting, cycling; and of course, boxing.

It has been said in pugilistic circles that Neiman has a great right hand. Dozens of fight posters and program covers bear his work. At big fights, he has long been a flamboyant presence in a front row seat; his Salvador-Dali-like mustache every bit as distinctive as Don King's hair.

"I had a mustache before I went into the army and they made me shave it off," LeRoy recounts. "It was a Clark Gable mustache. Clark Gable was one of my heroes. They don't have movie stars like that anymore. Anyway, after the war, I grew it back. Then, in the early 1960s, I had the same publisher as Salvador Dali. We spent some time together, and Dali's wife told me, 'Make up your mind; either cut it shorter or grow it out.' So I let it grow. Sometimes I tell people it's a virgin mustache, but that's not true. It's a prop, really. That's all."

Because of the mustache, LeRoy is easily recognizable in any setting. Stan Isaacs of Newsday once wrote, "Whether one approves of Neiman's work or not, one must agree that he himself is a work of art."

My own experience with LeRoy Neiman dates to 1989 when I interviewed him for a biography I was writing about Muhammad Ali. I arrived at his studio as per our appointment and was met with the question, "How do I know you're for real?"

Apparently, someone had recently interviewed LeRoy for what turned out to be a nonexistent project and walked out of his studio with several sketches. I produced a letter of authorization from Ali that I had brought with me for verification, and the interview began.

"I saw him in person for the first time in 1962," LeRoy reminisced, thinking back on his introduction to Muhammad. "It was when he fought Billy Daniels at St. Nick's Arena. I went back to this dingy dressing room, opened the door, and there was Ali—he was Cassius Clay then—sitting by himself on a table. I asked if I could draw him and he seemed to think that was a good idea, so I sat down and started to sketch. He was golden, no hair on his body, just beautiful. He looked like a piece of sculpture with no flaw or imperfection. His features and limbs were perfectly proportioned. He was an extraordinarily handsome charismatic man."

Over time, Neiman became a fixture at Ali fights. On one occasion in the dressing room before a bout, Ali asked his trainer Angelo Dundee to turn off the lights because he wanted to see if LeRoy could sketch in the dark.

Meanwhile, after interviewing LeRoy, I saw him frequently at fights and occasional social functions. He was always pleasant and polite. Despite his status in the world of art, he carried himself in a way that made him approachable. Thus, on the night of January 15, 2000, when Roy Jones fought David Telesco at Radio City Music Hall, I approached him with a request.

The University of Arkansas Press was about to publish a novel I had written entitled *Finding The Princess*. University presses are notoriously lacking in funds to publicize their books. And a sketch of the author by LeRoy Neiman on the back of the dust jacket would . . . Well, you get the picture.

LeRoy told me to call him at his studio on Monday. A week later, I was sitting in front of the master.

"It bothers me that people don't go to museums," LeRoy said as he sketched. "Painters read books. Maybe you can tell me; why don't more writers go to museums?" Ten minutes after starting, he decided that he didn't like the direction he was going in, put the first sheet of paper aside, and began anew . . . An orange pastel . . . Burnt umber . . . "Got to get the hair right," he said. "And I want a serious look."

Finding The Princess was published later that year. I smile whenever I look at the dust jacket.

Meanwhile, like Old Man River, LeRoy Neiman keeps rolling along. He is, simply put, the most commercially successful contemporary artist in America. His work is more popular now than ever. To his adoring followers, he can do no wrong. And his level of sustained activity is extraordinary.

LeRoy's artwork has appeared as etchings, sketches, lithographs, silkscreen prints, and paintings. Original Neiman paintings (acrylics, oil, or a mix) can be found for as little as $20,000 but most sell for multiples more. It costs in the neighborhood of $150,000 to commission a twenty-four-by-thirty-six-inch Neiman portrait. The eighteen-by-thirty-inch "study" he did for me as a favor would run roughly $10,000.

Some favor.

For over a quarter-century, LeRoy has created limited-edition serigraphs (silkscreen prints), which are distributed by Knoedler Publishing. These serigraphs are printed in limited editions (usually 250 to 500 copies), then numbered and signed by the artist. Six years ago, it was calculated that more than 150,000 LeRoy Neiman serigraphs had been purchased and that these prints had an estimated market value exceeding $400,000,000.

The numbers have gone higher since then.

Several years ago, Neiman created a six-by-four-foot "Athlete of the Century" painting of Muhammad Ali. One thousand limited-edition serigraphs were signed by Ali and the artist. Five hundred of the serigraphs had tiny additional drawings by LeRoy and Muhammad near the border and are now marketed at $8,000 each. The other five hundred are listed at $6,000. To date, over seven hundred "Athlete of the Century" serigraphs have been sold. Hammer Galleries, which handles much of Neiman's output, values the original painting at $2,000,000.

In truth, there has been criticism of Neiman's work. He has been called "the artist who critics love to hate" and "the most belittled artist of our time." Art critic Hilton Kramer was once asked to share a few thoughts on LeRoy Neiman and answered, "That might be difficult. I never think of him."

But the other side of the coin is that Neiman has brought art into more homes than any American artist ever. And it's worth noting that the Smithsonian Institution happily accepted the donation of his archives to its own Archives of American Art.

Thus, Neiman is able to say, "I get enough applause that I don't mind the negative things that are said and written about me. Maybe the critics are right, but what am I supposed to do about it? Stop painting? Change my work completely? I go into the studio. There I am at the easel. I enjoy what I'm doing and feel good working. If anyone tarnished my reputation as a serious artist, it was myself by playing around with *Playboy*. But I learned a lot from those folks, and I don't regret it." Then he adds, "I'm doing the best work of my life right now. I've never said that before, but now it's true. I've become more reflective."

So there you have it. I've sat on the sofa in my living room next to Muhammad Ali, watching tapes of Ali-Liston, the Rumble in the Jungle, and the Thrilla in Manila. I've walked eighteen holes with Arnold Palmer and been interviewed by Howard Cosell. Now I've had my likeness drawn by LeRoy Neiman. What more could any sports fan want?

Maybe someday Michael Jordan will shoot hoops with me.

On the third anniversary of Mickey Mantle's death, I reminisced about
"The Mick" for the New York Daily News.

Mickey Mantle:
A Personal Remembrance

In 1964, when I was eighteen years old, I met Mickey Mantle—sort of.

Mantle was in the fourteenth year of a glorious career that would see him hit 536 home runs, win three Most Valuable Player Awards, and play more games in a Yankee uniform than any other player ever.

I was a sophomore at Columbia University and hosted a weekly radio show called *Personalities In Sports* for the student-run radio station. Over the next few years, I would interview the likes of Joe Namath, Pete Rozelle, and Willis Reed; heady stuff for a kid barely out of high school. On this particular day, I'd brought my bulky reel-to-reel tape recorder to the Yankee dugout three hours before game time to tape my show.

Tom Tresh gave me my first interview; Whitey Ford, my second. Then Mantle entered the dugout. Gathering my courage, I approached him.

"Mr. Mantle. My name is Tom Hauser, and I wonder if I could interview you for WKCR."

"Fuck."

That was all he said. Not even "fuck you." Just "fuck," which I assumed meant "no," since he then turned and walked away from me.

Twenty-five years later, I again tried to interview Mantle. It was 1989; I was writing a biography of Muhammad Ali. To put Ali in perspective, I was speaking with other sports legends. My interview with Mantle had been scheduled in advance. And again he blew me off. Something about a bad hangover and "who gives a shit." We spoke briefly about Ali on the telephone a month later.

That history was on my mind as I walked down Central Park West toward Mickey Mantle's Restaurant and Sports Bar in 1994 for my third encounter with The Mick.

Mantle's life had taken some twists and turns during the preceding five years. His battles with alcoholism culminating in treatment at the Betty Ford Clinic were now public knowledge. His restaurant had become a midtown-Manhattan landmark. And he had launched a fantasy baseball camp in Florida.

The camp was the reason for our meeting. Mantle wanted me to write about it. And he was in an expansive mood as he talked about forty-five-year-old campers who were living out their dreams in often comical fashion. Then we touched on how he felt about New York in general, and he surprised me. He started to reminisce.

"When I first got here," Mantle recalled, "I lived with Hank Bauer in an apartment over the Stage Delicatessen. I didn't even own a suit. Hank was like a big brother to me. He took one look and said, 'We got to get you some clothes.' I lived with Hank during the season for a couple of years. Then I went out on my own and stayed at the St. Moritz."

Now The Quintessential Yankee was talking.

"There were two big advantages for me playing in New York. The first is that I was playing for the Yankees, and I liked being part of that tradition. Yankee Stadium is where Babe Ruth, Lou Gehrig, and Joe DiMaggio played. And the guys I played with were great. We had two catchers in the bullpen—Ralph Houk and Charlie Silvera—who would have started for any other team in the league. A lot of those Yankee teams I was on could have won it all just as easy without me. And the other advantage to playing in New York, although I didn't see it that way at the time, was the media. Hank Aaron was one of the greatest ballplayers who ever lived. You don't even need to look at home runs to know that. His lifetime batting average was higher than mine. He had more RBIs than anybody in history; more hits than anybody but Pete Rose and Ty Cobb; more runs than anybody except Ty Cobb and Babe Ruth. The Milwaukee Braves beat us in the World Series in 1957. But the question everybody always asked was, 'Who's greater, Willie Mays or me.' That's the power of the New York media."

As Mantle talked, I had the sense that he longed for a simpler time in his life, when everything revolved around fastballs and World Series triumphs. Still, he tried to put a good face on things.

"I might not be having as much fun as I used to," he said. "But I'm more at peace with myself now than before. And at least money isn't a problem. You know, I retired after the 1968 season, and the sports memorabilia craze hadn't started yet. For five years, it was like I'd died. I was never the smartest person in the world or the world's greatest businessman, so there were times when I was worried about whether or not I'd be able to take care of my family and myself."

Then Mantle thought again about happier times.

"New York has changed," he said. "I'll tell you a story that shows what I'm talking about. When I stayed at the St. Moritz, if the Yankees had a night game, I'd eat lunch outside the St. Moritz at that cafe they had on the sidewalk. Then Billy Martin and I would walk together through Central Park, up through Harlem, all the way to Yankee Stadium. No way you'd do that anymore."

We talked for an hour. Then I said good-bye.

After thirty years, I'd gotten my interview with Mickey Mantle.

Just after Marv Albert's comeback began, I spent some time with him for
a "Talk of the Town" piece in The New Yorker.

Marv Albert: "Yesss!"

At 10:25 on a brisk November night, a middle-aged man with a
familiar face stepped onto the set of a small television studio on the fourth
floor of Madison Square Garden. The man seemed a bit nervous. "I still
get butterflies before a show," he acknowledged. "But I think that's good.
If you lose that anxiety, you've lost your passion."

An attractive blonde applied a final touch of make-up.

A production assistant counted down the seconds.

At precisely 10:30, the man spoke in a nasal voice that was unmistak-
ably distinct and clear: "Good evening everyone. This is the Thursday
night edition of *National Finance SportsDesk*, and here is what's going on
tonight."

Marv Albert was on the air.

Albert is sports broadcasting royalty. He made his debut as a professional announcer in 1963 at age twenty-two. Not long after that, he
became the official voice of both the New York Knicks and Rangers.
Ultimately, his fame would rest on television, but his genius was, and still
is, most evident on radio.

Albert is able to describe fast-moving action as it unfolds before him.
There's perpetual emotion in his voice. In 1970, he earned a special place
in the hearts of New York sports fans with his dramatic call of the Knicks'
victory over the Los Angeles Lakers in the deciding game of the NBA
finals. It was the Knicks' first title ever. And because the game was blacked
out on television in the New York metropolitan area, Albert's radio audience was enormous.

For decades, Marv Albert seemed perpetually young and in love with
the games he called. He was a key figure in NBC's Olympic boxing coverage, a fixture on National Football League broadcasts, and the primary

play-by-play voice for six National Basketball Association finals. His signature "*Yesss!*"—sounded when a shot went in the basket—entered pop culture and transcended the game.

Then came his much publicized fall.

"My impeachment," Albert calls it. In September 1997, he pled guilty to misdemeanor sexual assault charges related to an incident that evolved out of a consensual relationship, resigned from his position at MSG Network, and was fired by NBC.

One year later, having undergone psychiatric counseling as per the terms of his "delayed sentence," Albert has seen his criminal conviction vacated and the charges against him dismissed. He has married his long-time fiancée and has a new perspective on life.

"My job was ideal for me," he says, looking back over the decades. "For years, before every game, I'd say to myself, 'There's no place I'd rather be.'" So of course, when I lost my job, I went through a phase of missing my work enormously. But then I got over it and began to enjoy the games as a fan. And after that, I started to see a lot of things differently. Before, I was always on the run, always getting ready for the next game. I never stopped to enjoy time with my family. Now I do. I'd never taken walks in Central Park. This past year, I discovered that walking in the park is fun. I'd always hated dogs; now I have two of them."

SportsDesk marks Albert's return to public life.

"My friends at The Garden stayed in touch during the past year," he recounts. "This summer, they asked if I was interested in coming back, and I was thrilled."

SportsDesk is a half-hour news show with an emphasis on New York sports. It's transmitted by the MSG cable network to parts of New York, New Jersey, Connecticut, and Pennsylvania.

In the past, Albert was known for being particularly well prepared as an announcer. "Doing my homework," he calls it. "You get consumed by it. Now that I'm working again, it's my whole day."

Five mornings a week, Albert has a telephone conversation with his producer. He reads sports sections from six newspapers. "It's almost a sickness," he acknowledges. Having recently gone online, he then pokes around in cyberspace for more sports to read. Most weekday afternoons, he arrives at his office by four o'clock. He writes his own copy for the show and likes it that way. The only disappointment attending his come-back to date is that he was also slated to call fifty Knicks games on WFAN radio, but the start of the season has been delayed by a bitter labor dispute. Meanwhile, MSG's ratings for *SportsDesk* have risen by 21 percent since he came onboard.

"There are times now when I'll be watching a major event like the NBA finals on television and I miss being there," Albert acknowledges. "But I don't view *SportsDesk* as a step backward. I tell myself that things are working out well. I love what I'm doing; I'm working hard; and I'm thankful to have my life back again. I'm making my comeback one step at a time."

This is a story that I began writing in 1985 and finished writing almost two decades later.

Pete Rose: A Meeting Remembered

After fourteen years of denying that he bet on baseball, Pete Rose now admits, not only that he bet on baseball but also that he bet on games involving teams that he managed. The admission comes in a book entitled *My Prison Without Bars*. Bud Selig, the commissioner of Major League Baseball, must now decide whether to lift the lifetime ban from the game imposed on Rose in 1989. That ban precludes Rose from being employed by any Major League team and also from being considered for induction into the Baseball Hall of Fame.

Rose was born on April 14, 1941, in the waning months of America's innocence before Pearl Harbor. It was the year Ted Williams, at age twenty-three, hit .406 and Joe DiMaggio hit safely in fifty-six consecutive games.

Pete Rose played baseball and football at Western Hills High School in Cincinnati, flunked tenth grade, and finally graduated. When he joined the Cincinnati Reds in 1963, a draconian reserve clause bound players to their teams at the whim of club owners. A black man had yet to win the Most Valuable Player Award in the American League. Many major league squads went south for spring training and stayed in segregated facilities.

Rose played through the terms of six presidents of the United States. He was far from being baseball's greatest hitter. But he might have been the sport's most persistent and durable good one.

As Rose's career progressed, the milestones passed one by one. He got the last hit in Cincinnati's old Crosley Field and the first hit by a member of the Reds in the new Riverfront Stadium. He was the National League's Rookie of the Year in 1963 and its Most Valuable Player ten years later. He played in six World Series.

In 1978, Rose equaled the National League mark set by Willie Keeler in 1897 by hitting safely in forty-four consecutive games. "I don't think you accomplish anything by tying someone," he said. The streak ended when Atlanta Braves reliever Gene Garber struck Rose out in the ninth inning of a 16–4 Atlanta rout. Garber refused to challenge Rose with fastballs, feeding him off-speed breaking pitches instead. After the game, Rose complained, "Garber was pitching like it was the seventh game of the World Series. If he had any guts, he'd have gone with his hard stuff." But Rose's complaint was sour grapes. The key to his own success was that he played every game and treated every at bat as though it were the seventh game of the World Series.

"Everybody wants a base hit when he goes up to bat," Mickey Mantle once said. "But with Pete, you always had the feeling that he wanted it more."

Rose retired as an active player in 1986, having played in more games and having had more at bats than anyone in the history of the game. He still ranks second in career doubles, fifth in runs scored, and sixth in total bases. But his greatest achievement was breaking a record that had been considered unsurpassable for more than fifty years.

On September 11, 1985, Rose lined a single to centerfield off San Diego pitcher Eric Show for the 4,192nd hit of his career. In so doing, he surpassed the mark emblazoned in baseball's record book by the immortal Ty Cobb.

Cobb's career began in 1905 when the American League was less than five years old. Automobiles were in their infancy. World War I was in the future and baseball was in its frontier days. In some ballparks, fans still stood behind ropes that were placed around the fringe of the field.

Cobb was only an average fielder with an ordinary arm. But he was a fiery competitor, obsessed with winning, whose play was marked by skill, daring, and fury. He had dazzling speed and was the greatest base runner of his time.

On the base paths, Cobb was aggressive and unpredictable, sliding as a matter of course with his spikes high. Three times during his career, he stole second, third, and home in the same inning. His 96 stolen bases in 1915 stood as the single-season record until Maury Wills stole 104 in 1962. His career record of 892 steals lasted until 1977, when it was surpassed by Lou Brock.

Writers who saw Cobb in his glory years chronicled his nature. Ken Smith described him as "an eagle swooping upon the baseball scene with spikes for talons." Jimmy Powers declared, "Cobb played the game ruth-lessly. The men in the field were his enemies. He would give them no quarter and he expected none." Robert Smith observed, "Cobb would slash a man with his spikes from hip to ankle if the man tried to block his path. Every opportunity at the plate or on base was to Cobb an individual contest between him and the pitcher, between him and the baseman, or between him and the whole wide world."

Cobb was more disliked than any other player in the game and had virtually no friends among his peers. In 1906, he had fistfights with four teammates: George Schmidt, Eddie Siever, George Mullin, and Sam Crawford. Even Babe Ruth, who was fond of most of his contemporaries, developed an intense dislike for Cobb; primarily because of his bench jockeying, which was inordinately cruel.

Cobb took his stance as a lefthander at bat. He would crowd home plate with his shoulders hunched forward, his hands several inches apart on the bat. To discourage pitchers who might otherwise throw at him, he perfected the drag bunt, putting the ball in play in a way that the first baseman would field it and the pitcher would have to cover first.

When Cobb retired in 1928, he had set ninety major league records and batted over .300 for twenty-three consecutive seasons. He led the American League in batting for nine years in a row (1907–1915); finished second to Tris Speaker in 1916 (.371 to .386); then led the league in bat-ting again for three more years (1917–1919).

For decades, Cobb held baseball's career records for games played, at bats, runs scored, RBIs, total bases, and stolen bases, and ranked second in doubles and triples. Seventy-five years after his retirement, he still ranks in the top-five in each of those categories.

But most significantly, Cobb compiled a career batting average of .367, which remains baseball's gold standard. And he amassed the extraor-dinary total of 4,191 base hits.

No other sport has records that are as carefully compiled and pre-served as baseball. These statistics are both the yardstick for measuring per-formance and the lifeblood of the game.

1985 was a banner year for baseball milestones. Rod Carew passed the three-thousand-hits mark. Nolan Ryan and Steve Carlton each notched his four thousandth strikeout. Tom Seaver, Phil Niekro, and Don Sutton surpassed three hundred wins. But that summer, Rose's quest for career hit number 4,192 dominated the game

I'd been writing for eight years by 1985. In late spring, I was invited to Cincinnati to meet with Rose and his attorney Reuven Katz. The baseball season was underway. Rose was approaching Cobb's record, and his agent was trying to put together a book deal. This would not be a definitive biography. Rather, it was seen as a narrowly focused work about breaking Cobb's mark.

Rose, Katz, and I met for lunch, and I was struck by Rose's appearance. He had heavy eyebrows, dark piercing eyes, and a granite-like jutting jaw. His bulky torso blended into a thick neck and heavy bulging thighs. In truth, he was inappropriately named. "Pete Bulldog" would have been better. Not a flower, and certainly not a rose.

I had heard it said that Rose was a baseball player first and a person second. Baseball was more than a job to him; it was his way of life. As we talked, that seemed to be true. He struck me as a man driven by forces that he didn't understand or care to understand. I also sensed that there was a lot of anger in him.

"I've won more games than any professional athlete ever," Rose told me. "Baseball, football, basketball, you name it. That's what it's all about, isn't it? I've walked off the field a winner more than nineteen hundred times. I've won more baseball games than forty-five Hall of Famers played in. I'm the winningest professional athlete ever."

"What about Willie Shoemaker?" I queried. "He has six thousand wins."

That earned me a dirty look and the rejoinder, "Yeah; but jockeys have eight or nine shots at winning every day."

I decided it would be unwise to mention that, going into the 1985 season, Rose had struck out 1,077 times and that, in addition to his thousands of hits, he had made more outs than any player in baseball history.

Meanwhile, as lunch progressed, Rose had a lot to say. One of the reasons for his popularity with writers was his quotability, and he was true to form that day.

"How many people do you know who went to college and don't make one-tenth as much money as I make? . . . I'd never want to be a pitcher. I wouldn't want to play a position where I could only play once every five days . . . Statistics are what let you look at a player who died before you were born and make him your hero . . . Millions of Americans have fantasized about breaking Ty Cobb's record. But I'm the one who's doing it."

After lunch, Rose went to the ballpark and Katz suggested that I accompany him back to his office to further discuss the book. The project interested me. I was a baseball fan. I admired Rose's accomplishments. This would be an opportunity to experience a historic moment from a unique perspective. The book would be short. It would be written in narrative about, not by, its subject. Katz would see to it that I was given full media privileges, and I'd have regular access to Rose.

"I like you," Katz said. "I think Pete feels comfortable with you. If the dollars can be worked out, I'd like to go ahead with the book, but there's something we have to discuss first."

I waited.

"I'm familiar with your work," Katz continued. "I know the kind of research you do. If we go ahead on this, you're going to learn that there are many sides to Pete Rose. Pete knows a lot of women in a lot of towns. He's also a gambler. He bets and loses a lot more than he should. Most of that is at the track but not all of it. I don't want any of that in the book. This has to be about Pete as a baseball player breaking Ty Cobb's record. If you're not comfortable with that, I'll have full respect for you but we'll have to find another writer."

I told Katz that his conditions were acceptable. We were contemplating a narrowly focused book; not a definitive biography. Ultimately, the project didn't go ahead because the dollars weren't there. But before Katz and I said good-bye, I had a question to ask.

"Does Pete bet on baseball?"

Katz looked me right in the eye. "I hope not," he said.

That brings us to the issues at hand: "Should Pete Rose be allowed to hold a job in Major League Baseball again? And should he be eligible for induction into the Hall of Fame?"

For a player or manager to gamble on baseball, particularly on games in which he's involved, is the sport's cardinal sin.

Rule 21(d) of the Rules of Major League Baseball declares: "Any player, umpire, or club official or employee, who shall bet any sum whatsoever upon any baseball game in connection with which the bettor has no duty to perform shall be declared ineligible for one year. Any player, umpire, or club or league official or employee, who shall bet any sum whatsoever upon any baseball game in connection with which the bettor has a duty to perform shall be declared permanently ineligible."

A report compiled for Major League Baseball by John Dowd in 1989 concluded that Rose made at least 412 wagers on baseball games between April 8, 1985, and July 5, 1987. According to Dowd, 52 of those wagers were on teams that Rose played on and/or managed.

As a baseball player, Rose was pure. No major leaguer ever played closer to his full potential. Rose's 4,256 hits stand testament to that. But "permanently ineligible" means permanently ineligible. A lifetime ban should only be lifted for good cause.

Rose's lack of contrition with regard to his wrongdoing is troubling. Even now, in his book, he declares, "I'm sure that I'm supposed to act all sorry or sad or guilty now that I've accepted that I've done something wrong. But you see, I'm just not built that way."

In other words, the only thing Rose seems sorry about is that he has been caught and punished.

It should also be noted that Rose's admission that he bet on baseball games while playing and managing in the major leagues came in a for-profit mode. He received a reported one-million-dollar advance for his new book. By contrast, in a previous autobiography published in 1989, he denied having bet on baseball.

The thought of Rose being employed again in Major League Baseball is troubling. Given his history, no matter what he says now, there's no way to know that he won't bet on baseball in the future. And his reinstatement would send a mixed message with regard to how forcefully baseball intends to protect the integrity of the game in the years ahead.

In sum, there's more to be done before reinstatement is appropriate. This shouldn't be a matter of Rose saying, "Okay; after fourteen years of lying, a publisher paid me a million dollars to admit that I bet on baseball, so let me back in."

At the very least, Rose's sincerity and candor should be further tested. Let him openly discuss all facets of his wrongdoing with the media and others. Then, two years from now, if his conduct so warrants, the commissioner can reconsider whether to allow him back into the game. There's no need to rush to judgment.

As for the Hall of Fame; a player has twenty years after he has last played in the Major Leagues to be elected by America's baseball writers. To be inducted, he must be named on 75 percent of the approximately five hundred ballots cast. If Rose were reinstated now, December 2004 and December 2005 would be the last two years in which he is eligible for regular induction. Thereafter, he would need to be named on 75 percent of the ballots cast by a veterans committee comprised of all living members of the Hall of Fame and the winners of certain awards for writing and broadcasting.

The same two-year waiting period should be applied before reconsideration of Rose's eligibility for induction into the Hall of Fame. Then, if he has truly reformed, whether or not he is inducted should be determined, not by baseball writers, but by his true peers.

As the 2005 season began, Major League Baseball faced a scandal of a different kind.

Baseball's Steroid Problem

Recent reports of steroid use by Major League Baseball players are shadowing the start of the 2005 season. A federal grand jury has heard testimony regarding alleged steroid use by Barry Bonds, Gary Sheffield, and Jason Giambi. Jose Conseco claims in a new book to have shot up with Mark McGwire. Some of the allegations might be unfounded, but it's clear that the presence of steroids in baseball constitutes a significant problem.

Let's start by noting that allegations of steroid use aren't new. They surfaced in the late 1980s and gathered steam in 1998, when McGwire and Sammy Sosa vied to become baseball's new single-season home-run king. McGwire acknowledged using a natural hormone called androstenedione, which is favored by body-builders and has since has been banned by Major League Baseball. Sosa denied steroid use, but his body changed in remarkable ways. Meanwhile, Bonds was growing from a 185-pound leadoff hitter into a 230-pound behemoth. After hitting a career-high forty-nine home runs in 2000, he smashed seventy-three round-trippers in 2001.

Then, in June 2002, Tom Verducci authored a groundbreaking expose for *Sports Illustrated*. "Steroid use, which a decade ago was considered a taboo violated by a few renegade sluggers," Verducci wrote, "is now so rampant in baseball that even pitchers and wispy outfielders are juicing up and talking openly among themselves about it."

Verducci described the game as a "pharmacological trade show" with hundreds of players relying on illegal performance-enhancing drugs. He quoted Curt Schilling as saying, "I'll pat guys on the ass [baseball's traditional slap on the butt for a job well-done], and they'll look at me and go, 'Don't hit me there, man. It hurts.' That's where they shoot the steroid needles. You look at some of these players and you know what's going on.

Guys out there look like Mr. Potato Head, with a head and arms and six or seven body parts that just don't look right. They don't fit."

Verducci also reported on former All-Star Ken Caminiti, who acknowledged winning the 1996 National League Most Valuable Player award while on steroids.

"I've made a ton of mistakes," Verducci quoted Caminiti as saying, "but I don't think using steroids is one of them. It's no secret what's going on in baseball. At least half the guys are using steroids. They talk about it. They joke about it with each other. The guys who want to protect themselves or their image by lying have that right. Me? I don't want to hurt teammates or friends, but I've got nothing to hide. If a young player were to ask me what to do, I'm not going to tell him it's bad. Look at all the money in the game. You have a chance to set your family up, to get your daughter into a better school. So I can't say, 'Don't do it.' Not when the guy next to you is as big as a house, and he's going to take your job and make the money."

Major League Baseball's response to Verducci's revelations was a resounding nothing. Commissioner Bud Selig and his owner-brethren largely ignored the issue. Bonds, who insisted that he had added muscle exclusively through proper diet and training, told the Associated Press, "What players take doesn't matter. It's nobody else's business. The doctors should spend their time looking for cures for cancer."

Then came a crisis that couldn't be swept under the rug. In February 2004, a federal grand jury in San Francisco handed down indictments charging four men with the illegal distribution of steroids and other performance-enhancing substances. Among the indicted were Victor Conte and Greg Anderson.

Conte had founded the Bay Area Laboratory Co-Operative (BALCO), a medical facility that specialized in testing athletes and providing them with "nutritional supplements" through a subsidiary known as SNAC (Scientific Nutrition for Advanced Conditioning).

Anderson is a longtime friend of Bonds and had begun working with the star as his personal trainer in 1998. The site of their workouts was a gym located one block from BALCO. Anderson introduced Bonds to Conte, who arranged for a nutritional supplement plan.

When federal authorities raided BALCO in September 2003, they reportedly found client lists, steroids, and human growth hormone. It was also reported by the *San Francisco Chronicle* that a raid of Anderson's apartment resulted in the seizure of steroids, sixty thousand dollars in cash, and documents detailing the use of performance-enhancing drugs by various athletes.

The Chronicle further revealed that Bonds had testified before a federal grand jury and admitted that he had "unknowingly" used steroids provided by Anderson during the 2003 season. More specifically, Bonds said that he had received and used two substances known as "the clear" and "the cream" after being told by Anderson that they were flaxseed oil and a rubbing balm for arthritis. During Bonds's testimony, prosecutors showed him documents from 2001, 2002, and 2003, indicating that he had used human growth hormone, depo-testosterone, insulin, and Clomid (a female infertility drug that enhances the effect of testosterone).

Conte's response to the indictments has been defiance. "It's not cheating if everybody is doing it," he said last December. "If you've got knowledge of what everyone is doing and those are the real rules of the game, then you're not cheating."

Bonds has been a bit more coy, as evidenced by the following dialogue at a February 22, 2005, press conference:

Question: Can you explain over the last four or five years your amazing production, your tremendous growth in muscle strength, getting stronger as you get older?

Bonds: Hard work. That's about it.

Q: Do you personally think that steroids have been a part of baseball in the last fifteen or so years?

Bonds: You know what; truthfully, I never really paid any attention to it, nor did I really care because I worry about me. That's it. I was good then and I'm still good.

Q: Do you view the use of steroids as cheating?

Bonds: Cheating? I don't know what cheating is. I don't know if steroids are going to help you in baseball. I just don't believe it. I don't believe steroids can help you, eye-hand coordination, technically hit a baseball. I just don't believe it.

Meanwhile, the United States Congress has gotten into the act with a flurry of subpoenas served upon players, former players, and Major League Baseball executives.

So what's the fuss about? Players compete with fused bone and screws in their limbs. The use of nutritional supplements is encouraged. Why are steroids different?

Let's begin by stating the obvious. Steroids do work. When used in conjunction with vigorous physical training and increased protein intake, they promote the development of muscle tissue and result in an increased capacity to train and compete. It's no accident that Jason Giambi, Jose Conseco, and Ken Caminiti (all admitted steroid users) each won an MVP award after going on "the juice." Barry Bonds has won seven MVP awards, including four in a row (2001–2004) after documents in the possession of prosecutors indicate that he began using human growth hormone and steroids.

So let's rephrase the question: Why is steroid use by Major League Baseball players bad?

For starters, unless prescribed by a doctor for an existing medical condition, steroid use is illegal in the United States. And as a general rule, the law should be followed.

Steroids give users an unfair competitive advantage over those who abstain.

And there are health issues. Dr. Nieca Goldberg (a spokesperson for the American Heart Association) declares, "Steroids raise nearly all heart disease risk factors. Steroid use raises blood pressure. It makes the arteries vulnerable since, because of elevated cholesterol, you get cholesterol plaque buildup. Steroid abuse can also cause a dangerous thickening of heart muscle called hypertrophy; the same kind of heart-muscle enlargement seen in patients with congestive heart failure."

Todd Chapman (a cardiac surgeon in Nevada and member of the medical advisory board for the Nevada State Athletic Commission) concurs and says, "Add to that the clot forming effect of steroids and you have a recipe for a stroke. The liver doesn't fare much better. Liver tumors and cysts are seen with increased frequency in steroid users. Girls might like the muscles, but they won't be impressed by the raging acne, male pattern baldness, shrunken testicles, and gynecomastia (breast enlargement in males). And if your wife wants a family, she might have to look for a sperm donor because steroids increase the chances of being sterile."

That dovetails with Ken Caminiti's experience. By the end of the 1996 season, his testicles had shrunk and his body had all but stopped producing its own testosterone.

And perhaps most pernicious of all, professional athletes are role models. Young men and women watch what their heroes do and often follow suit. A recent study by the National Institute on Drug Abuse concluded that 3.4 percent of twelfth graders in the United States have used steroids. More alarmingly, in 1992, 71 percent of high-school seniors perceived steroid use as harmful. In 2004, that number had dropped to 55 percent.

Meanwhile, Major League Baseball remains in denial. The owners and players union have agreed to conduct limited steroid testing. But even now, the penalties are minimal: a ten-day suspension for the first positive test OR a fine of up to $10,000; thirty days for the second positive test; and sixty days for the third. A player must test positive for illegal steroid use on four occasions before he's suspended for a full season. And the use of human growth hormone isn't banned.

The union says it's protecting its members and doesn't want to set a precedent for future negotiations regarding other drugs like cocaine and marijuana. But the union is misguided. Baseball's owners don't care about the health of their players. They regard illegal steroid use as an image problem. The players, unless they're morons, should take a different view.

Years ago, the Major League Baseball players union took the lead among major sports in elevating player salaries. Now it should do the same with regard to the health of its members. The standard rationale for steroid use in baseball is, "So many other players are doing it that I have to do it to compete."

So level the playing field. It's a no-brainer. Eradicate illegal steroid use from baseball. Institute mandatory anytime testing. The first violation by a player should result in a one-year suspension; the second in a lifetime ban.

Very few baseball players bet on baseball today. Why not? Because they know that if they do and get caught, they'll be banned for life. That's the lesson of Pete Rose.

Like gambling, steroids threaten the integrity of baseball. But worse, they endanger players' lives. A true "get-tough" policy on steroids would safeguard the lives of Major League Baseball players and also of thousands of young men and women who emulate them.

Hank Aaron, Willie Mays, and their brethren didn't need steroids to have long careers and be great. As for Ken Caminiti, one would like to know his opinion on the subject today but that's impossible. He died of a heart attack last October at age forty-one.

In 2009, I revisited Columbia football.

In the Press Box

Let's get the bad stuff out of the way first. Entering the 2009 season, the Columbia football team had lost 605 games. Only two teams in college football history—Northwestern (614 losses) and VMI (612)—have lost more. The last Columbia coach to compile a winning record was Charles Crowley, who relinquished the reins in 1929.

The first Columbia football game I saw was the home opener against Princeton in 1963. In the forty-six years that I've been following Columbia football, the Lions have had three winning seasons. During that time, their record has been 103 victories, 330 defeats, and 9 ties. Discounting the ties, that comes to a .238 winning percentage. This is not good.

On the plus side; Baker Field is a nice place to watch a football game. Tickets are always available. And the Lions are true student athletes. Football is an extracurricular activity at Columbia; not an obsession. The players play because they love the game.

During my years as a student at Columbia, I went to all but one home game. Now I go to one game a year and listen to several more on WKCR. My sport of choice has become boxing. As a writer, I've covered hundreds of fights from ringside. I realized this summer that, for all the times I'd seen the Lions play football, I'd never been in the press box for a Columbia game. I decided to fill that void in my life by writing about this year's home opener against Central Connecticut State.

September 26 was a perfect day for football. Blue sky, a gentle breeze, temperature in the mid-sixties. On a day like that, there's no nicer place to watch a game than Robert K. Kraft Field in Lawrence A. Wein Stadium at the Baker Athletics Complex.

The press room at Wein Stadium overlooks the field from high above the back row of the stands. A long built-in table and sixteen chairs are set against a windowed wall that offers a panoramic view of the field. A second table and ten chairs stand on a platform close behind.

There had been twenty-seven requests for press credentials. I was seated in the front row overlooking the fifty-yard-line. Major media was largely absent. The *Columbia Daily Spectator* was well represented, as were several college-football Internet sites. Most of the reporters were of student age. I was one of the few with gray hair. I was also one of the few writing longhand on a yellow pad. Laptops were the preferred means of note taking. There was wireless Internet access.

Muffins, bagels, fresh fruit, and bottled beverages were set out on a table at the north end of the room. Copies of the Columbia football media guide and the day's game program were also available.

This was the first meeting on the gridiron between Columbia and Central Connecticut State. One cynic suggested that CCS doesn't really have a football team; that their coach went through the dorms on Thursday night asking, "Does anyone want to play Columbia in football on Saturday?"

In reality, Central Connecticut State had a 4-and-3 record in Northeast conference play last year (losing to Albany, Monmouth, and Robert Morris). It had split its first two games of the 2009 campaign.

Columbia had won its 2009 season opener against Fordham 40–28 and was bidding to win its first two games for the fifth time in fifty-seven years.

The game began at 12:30. Columbia returned the opening kick to its own forty-four-yard line. A face-mask penalty against Central Connecticut State, a twenty-eight-yard pass from M. A. Olawale to Joseph Taylor, and three well-executed rushes by Ray Rangel followed. Seventy-six seconds into the game, the Lions led 7–0.

Three minutes later, Columbia had the ball again, pinned inside its own one-yard line. Rangel for forty-nine yards on first down. Rangel for thirty-four yards on first down. First and ten Columbia on the Central Connecticut State seventeen. The Lions looked like Ohio State.

Then the drive sputtered. A Columbia field goal attempt was blocked. Late in the quarter, Central Connecticut State blocked a punt and recovered at the Lions one-yard line. A heroic defensive stand stopped them cold.

At the end of the first quarter, the Lions led 7–0. Darlene Camacho (Columbia's director of sports information and media relations) and her staff passed out statistical summaries, as they would throughout the afternoon.

The second quarter began with an extension of hope. An eleven-yard-pass from Olawale to Austin Knowlin gave Columbia a 13–0 lead. But Central Connecticut State blocked the extra-point attempt (its third blocked kick of the half) and returned the ball the length of the field for two points. The Lions led 13 to 2, but I was starting to feel uneasy. I'd seen this tragedy acted out before.

Late in the second quarter, Central Connecticut State narrowed the margin to 13–9. Just before halftime, an athletic department intern came through the room asking each of the writers if we'd like a turkey, tuna, chicken salad, or Caesar wrap.

The wraps were good, as were the chips and cookies that came with them. But in truth, I would have rather been in the stands. The press box is obviously a fantastic place to be when it's twenty degrees outside and the wind is whipping in off the Spuyten Duyvil. But on a warm sunny day, it's more satisfying to sit close to the action, surrounded by cheering fans and in close proximity to the Columbia band.

All I'll say about the second half is that it had a sadly familiar ring. Central Connecticut State scored thirteen unanswered points for a 22–13 win.

After the game, the media was offered an opportunity to meet with some of the players and the head coach of each team. Nine of us made the trip to the second floor of the Chrystie Fieldhouse.

Central Connecticut State head coach Jeff McInerney spoke first. He called Columbia "a traditional Ivy League power" and said that Lions head coach Norries Wilson was "a great coach who will win a lot of games."

CCS quarterback Aubrey Norris (who'd completed eight of eight passes for 135 yards and rushed ten times for another 79) was asked what he thought of Columbia.

"I don't think they were tackling that well," he answered.

That assessment was echoed later by Coach Wilson, who declared, "They came out in the second half and stuffed it right in our faces."

Then Wilson was asked why it has been so difficult over the years to turn Columbia's football fortunes around.

"I don't know," he said with a shrug. "Snowballs roll in two directions. They can roll bad or they can roll good. We got to find a way to turn the snowball around."

It has been a long time since Columbia beat Stanford 7–0 in the 1934 Rose Bowl. Gridiron glory of that magnitude is unlikely to come to Morningside Heights again. But those of us with Columbia blue in our blood will continue to root for the Lions on the gridiron the way we once rooted for Charlie Brown in *Peanuts*. Wherever we are when they take the field, our hearts will be with them.

This was an exercise in watching a basketball game through different eyes.

Courtside with David Diamante

Boxing fans know David Diamante as a guy with dreadlocks that reach below his waist and as one of the best ring announcers in the business. The sweet science is his first love. But recently, it has been his secondary gig.

Since the start of the 2011–12 NBA season, Diamante has been the in-arena voice of the New Jersey Nets.

Last fall, David read an article about the Nets holding auditions for a new PA announcer. He applied for the position, went through a rigorous audition process, and got the job. Then, like everyone else, he waited through a contract dispute between the owners and players that delayed the start of the NBA season until December 25.

"It was tough sitting out the lockout," Diamante says, "although I'm sure it was tougher for the players and a lot of other people associated with the Nets. It was a great Christmas present for me when everything was settled and the games started. I'm passionate about sports. Boxing is my favorite; I want to announce fights forever. But I love basketball and I love doing this. I've got a multi-year contract with the Nets, which means I can put all of my energy and emotion into doing the job right rather than worrying about whether or not I'll he hired to work the next fight."

This season has tested the loyalty of Nets fans. Brook Lopez (the team's elite center) has been sidelined with a foot injury. Point guard Deron Williams is the squad's best player, but power forward Kris Humphries is the most famous by virtue of his ill-fated marriage to Kim Kardashian. The Nets didn't win at home until their fifteenth game; a 107–100 triumph over Golden State. And it's a matter of record that the team will move across the Hudson River to Barclays Center in Brooklyn after the 2011–12 season.

Diamante is responsible for creating an air of optimism in the here and now at the Prudential Center in Newark, where the Nets play their home games.

"I felt comfortable in the job from the start," David says. "That's partly because I'm backed by good people who give me great support. And some of the jobs I had before this, like working in clubs where anything can happen, means that the unexpected never shakes me."

"And I love the job," Diamante continues. "I'm a boxing guy. When you're boxing and someone hits you in the nose and you feel the bone crunch and you taste your own blood, you can't call 'time out.' But there's a lot of physical contact in basketball. These guys are big; these guys are strong; and there are times when they beat each other up. Taking a charge in the NBA is like getting punched in the body by a heavyweight. And when a basketball player falls, it's on a hard wood court, not a ring canvas. The best basketball players have the same killer instinct that fighters have. They'll pay any price to win. And seeing them up close, you realize what amazing athletes they are. You can't really see how good they are on television. But to sit at the edge of the court and watch them whiz by on a fast break; for men that big to move that fast with such agility is extraordinary. And it's beautiful to see them work together as a team."

On Sunday, January 29, Diamante arrived at the Prudential Center at 4:00 PM. Wearing a navy-blue suit, striped shirt, and conservative tie, he moved easily through the back passageways of the arena, offering a warm hello to everyone he passed.

The Nets would be playing the Toronto Raptors. Game time was 6:05 PM. New Jersey had a 7-and-13 record, but was coming into the contest on a two-game winning streak. The Raptors sported a 6-and-14 ledger and were without their leading scorer, seven-foot center Andrea Bargnani.

Diamante does his homework assiduously. He watches all of the Nets away games on television and researches upcoming opponents on the Internet. He's constantly running inventive phrases through his mind. A three-point field goal for Deron Williams becomes a "three-Will" for D-Will. Alone at home, he rehearses calls to see how they sound and feel.

In the press room, David picked up a media packet and began highlighting names with a yellow marker.

The Nets have four players whose surname is Williams: Deron Williams, Sheldon Williams, Jordan Williams, and Shawne Williams.

"If I miss a play," Diamante noted, "I can call 'Williams' and have a pretty good chance of getting it right."

When his review was done, David ate a light dinner (there was a buffet for staff and working press). At 5:15, he entered the arena and took his place at a long table midway between the Nets and Raptors benches.

"Ladies and gentlemen," he intoned, "welcome to the Prudential Center, home of Nets basketball."

Over the next half-hour, Diamante offered a stream of information to those in attendance. He thanked various Nets sponsors; talked about ticket packages for upcoming games; warned against smoking in the arena; and welcomed a group of students from the Willard School in Ridgewood, New Jersey. In due course, he was joined at the table by the timekeeper, head scorer, and announcers for the YES television network.

At 5:47, the Raptors took the floor to warm up . . . "Ladies and gentlemen; please welcome tonight's opponent, the Toronto Raptors."

The Nets followed a minute later . . . "Ladies and gentlemen, please welcome your NEW . . . JERSEY . . . NETS !!!!!"

"In boxing," Diamante notes, "I'm expected to be impartial. Here, it's part of my job to be a Nets fan. I'm always respectful toward the other team. But when one of our guys scores, I don't just say it; I sing it."

At 6:05, Diamante introduced the Raptors starting line-up. Then—

Lights out . . . Spotlights . . . Pulsating music . . .

"The starting line-up for your NEW . . . JERSEY . . . NETS !!!!!"

And finally, Diamante's signature line ("the fight starts now"), modified for basketball.

"And now, ladies and gentlemen; from the four corners of the world to the four corners of this court, *the game starts now.*"

Tip-off . . . The Nets controlled the ball.

"Being the PA announcer for an NBA team requires a different skill set from ring announcing," Diamante explains. "In boxing, there are times when I'm in the center of the ring reading the decision after a close fight and millions of people are hanging on my every word. Here, the focus is never on me. I'm heard but not seen. And unlike ring announcing, where I'm only on at the beginning and end of a fight, I'm calling the entire game for the crowd. There's no downtime, no time to daydream. I have to pay close attention every second of the game."

As the game progressed, Diamante catalogued the action, calling out the name of each player who scored and more.

"Traveling . . . Time out, Nets . . . Checking in for Toronto, number eleven . . . Please welcome the Nets dancers . . ."

At the end of the first quarter, the score was tied at 24. Toronto had a 44–39 lead at the half. A 10–2 spurt put the Raptors up by 13 points early in the third stanza. The Nets trailed by 17 at the three-quarter mark. With 7:24 left in the game and the Raptors ahead 82 to 62, the crowd began filing out.

At 8:15 PM, it was over. The Nets had lost a game that, on paper, they should have won. Final score: Raptors 94, Nets 73.

Diamante announced that Deron Williams was high scorer for the Nets with 24 points; then closed with, "Thank you for coming. And please, arrive home safely."

Thomas Wolfe once wrote You Can't Go Home Again. *But you can.*

I Could Always Hit a Baseball

Baseball might no longer be America's national pastime, but it's still deeply ingrained in the fabric of America.

Robert Frost wrote, "Some baseball is the fate of us all. For my part, I am never more at home in America than at a baseball game."

Jacques Barzun added, "Whoever would understand the heart and mind of America had better learn baseball."

Baseball is also deeply ingrained in memories of childhood. Unlike a football or basketball, a baseball is manageable in a child's hand.

I grew up in a house with a backyard that was shaped like Yankee Stadium. My childhood was spent playing baseball using imaginary runners with three kids on a side. When only one friend was available, we'd play whiffle ball or stickball with a huge boulder as a backstop.

I wasn't a gifted athlete. But for whatever reason, at whatever level I played, I could always hit a baseball. From age seven through high school, hardball was my game. I played softball in college and thereafter.

Like most children who love sports, I enjoyed occasional moments of glory. There were crucial hits in heated rivalries and season-ending championship wins. But the greatest satisfaction came from the wonderful harmonic feeling of hitting a baseball well. I was a line-drive hitter; mostly singles and doubles. And there were times when my bat felt like a magic wand in my hands.

Once, on a warm August night when I was twenty-one years old, I was playing first base in an unimportant encounter between counselors from two day camps. Midway through the game, I lined a single to left field to drive in the go-ahead run. I remember very clearly rounding first base, pulling up after making the turn, and thinking, "What a glorious feeling, to be playing baseball on a night like tonight."

But as I got older, I found myself playing less and less. The last time I stepped onto a diamond was 1977, when I was thirty-one years old. Earlier this year, I realized that it had been twenty-seven years since I hit a baseball. And a thought that wouldn't go away entered my mind. I wanted to enlist a pitcher, go to the park, and see what skills remained.

I mentioned my plan to Tim McCarver, the all-star catcher whose career with the St. Louis Cardinals and Philadelphia Phillies ended in 1980. McCarver is one of baseball's best analytical minds and among the sport's finest television commentators.

"There's something you should understand," McCarver told me. "Hitting a baseball isn't like riding a bike. Your body forgets. Believe me; I know of whence I speak."

McCarver then recounted for me a humbling experience that occurred in 1991 when sixty-four-year-old Los Angeles Dodgers manager Tommy Lasorda goaded him into taking some swings during batting practice. Lasorda once pitched in the major leagues, compiling a career record of no wins and four losses with an earned run average of 6.48. McCarver had batted .478 for the victorious Cardinals in the 1964 World Series and, thirteen years later, averaged .320 for a full season at age thirty-five.

"But against Tommy," McCarver reminisced, "the results were not what I had hoped for."

Properly warned, I resolved to proceed as planned.

Judgment Day came. I went to a closet in my apartment and took out three wood bats; each of them about forty years old. Then I found an old softball; put on jogging shoes, black sweatpants, and a black T-shirt; and set out for the baseball fields off Fifth Avenue at 100th Street in Central Park.

As a kid, I'd loved every at bat; particularly in pressure situations. Nothing pleased me more than going to the plate in the bottom of the ninth inning with the tying and winning runs on base. Now, for the first time, I was apprehensive about hitting a baseball. I was afraid of failing, and it crossed my mind that my grand experiment could be cut short by a pulled muscle or worse. It was possible that I would return home feeling like a very old fifty-eight-year-old man.

The field in Central Park was well manicured and green. The pitcher was Casey Simons; a thirteen-year-old student at Simon Baruch Middle School in Manhattan, who will be entering Brooklyn Tech this autumn. Casey's father, Josh, graciously agreed to chase down any balls I might hit.

"Let's start with slow-pitch softball," I suggested.

That seemed to disappoint Casey, who had an official Little League hardball with him and seemed anxious to blow me away with his good stuff. But being a nice young man, he complied.

The first pitch came in, and I lofted a pop-up to shortstop.

Next pitch.

Whack !

A line drive to left field.

"This could turn out better than I thought," I thought.

Base hit up the middle.

Pop up to third base.

Line drive in fair territory down the left-field line.

Another pop up.

My timing wasn't great; but the pitches were slow and I was starting to remember the mental part of hitting . . . Wait for your pitch . . . Don't swing at a pitch just because it's a strike unless there are two strikes on you . . . Only try to pull the ball when it's on the inside half of the plate.

Josh moved deeper into left field and I smashed a line drive into the gap.

"Dive for it, Dad," Casey shouted.

Discretion being the better part of valor, Josh didn't.

"A double," Casey conceded.

I took about twenty swings and, to my delight, whiffed only once.

Then it was time for hardball.

Here I should note that Casey is the ace pitcher for the Orioles in the junior division of the Greenwich Village Little League. His repertoire includes a fastball, two-seam fastball, four-seam fastball, curveball, knuckle-curve, and change-up.

"How about just showing me the change-up," I suggested. "Think batting practice; not seventh game of the World Series."

The hardball was harder to hit than the softball.

Pop up.

Swing and a miss.

Swing and a miss.

WHACK ! ! !

A line drive rocketed off my bat toward the trees in deep left field. And suddenly, I was young again.

"Okay," I told Casey. "Now you can throw your good stuff."

Thereafter, to quote Tim McCarver, "The results were not what I had hoped for."

Still—

"I was surprised," Casey told me when we were done. "Your timing could be better, but you got around on a few of them." He politely avoided mentioning that, toward the end, I was breathing hard and that I fell down on one of my swings.

Now, as I type these remembrances, the experience of hitting a base-ball is very much on my mind. I have large blisters on the inside of both thumbs and a third blister at the base of the index finger on my left hand. But there's satisfaction in knowing that I can still hit a line drive into the gap in left center field. The ball might not travel as far as it once did, but my memories have been renewed.

Maybe this autumn, I'll toss a football around in the park.

Life goes on. Life goes by.

Destroying the High Temple

For thousands of years, the most physically imposing buildings on earth were temples, churches, and mosques. In the twentieth century, new houses of worship came to dominate the landscape.

Yankee Stadium is the most storied of these contemporary shrines. When it opened in 1923, baseball was in the shadow of the 1919 Black Sox Scandal, and the wounds from the long war between the American and National leagues had yet to fully heal.

The Yankees' new home was the first baseball facility to be called a "stadium." In ensuing years, the team and Babe Ruth captured the imagination of America. Stadium lore became intertwined with Lou Gehrig and Joe DiMaggio; the Baltimore Colts beating the New York Giants in the most important football game ever played; Sugar Ray Robinson wilting in the heat against Joey Maxim; and Joe Louis's annihilation of Max Schmeling.

In 1946, the year I was born, Yankee Stadium was only twenty-three years old. But from my perspective as a boy, it had been around forever. At age seven, I saw it for the first time. As I grew older and was allowed to navigate New York City's subway system on my own, I went to Sunday doubleheaders with friends on a regular basis.

Three of my childhood dreams went unfulfilled. I never saw a no-hitter; never saw a triple play; and never caught a ball that had been hit into the stands. But I did see the Yankees beat the Brooklyn Dodgers in a World Series game when I was ten. I watched Mickey Mantle and Roger Maris hit home runs in 1961. And I took pride in the fact that the stadium was impregnable. No one ever hit a fair ball out of it.

In the mid-1970s, Yankee Stadium was renovated. Steel columns that supported the roof and upper decks (and obstructed a clear view of the field from some seats) were removed. When the renovation was complete, the copper facade that ran along the edge of the roof and was synonymous with the stadium was gone. The colors were different too. The familiar aquamarine seats and surrounding environs had been replaced by a pedestrian blue.

But by then, my sojourns to Yankee Stadium had become less frequent. Visiting the stadium had taken on the feel of going back to a highschool reunion; seeing a girl I'd longed for when I was young; and realizing that, with the passage of time, she was far less enticing. Baseball as I'd known it as a boy was gone. And I'd changed too.

Still, it's discomforting to me that Yankee Stadium (which has been in existence longer than many countries in the world today) is about to be torn down.

Who wants a new Yankee Stadium? Not the fans. They like it the way it is. The Yankees have led the league in attendance for five consecutive seasons. Home attendance in 2007 was 4,271,867; an average of 52,739 per game.

The new stadium, of course, is driven by economics. The 1970s renovation has been fully depreciated for tax purposes. And while the Yankees talk about creating a more "fan-friendly" environment, the "improvements" (like amenities in a Las Vegas hotel-casino) will be all about separating people from their money.

The original Yankee Stadium cost $2,500,000 to build. The new stadium will cost in excess of $1.2 billion dollars. One way or another, much of that total will be borne by the taxpayers of the City of New York.

The original stadium once seated 71,699 fans for baseball. Its current capacity is 57,545. The new stadium will accommodate 55,000. More significantly, it will be constructed in a way that positions the most expensive suites at field level.

That's like the Vatican tearing down St. Peter's Basilica to build a new house of worship with a Jumbotron and luxury pews.

The new Yankee Stadium will have 1,800 "legends" seats at prices ranging from $2,500 to $500 per seat per game. Those prices are obscene.

Alternatively, season-ticket holders can choose from 1,200 seats at $350 per ticket or 1,300 seats at prices ranging from $135 to $100. There will also be 48,000 "non-premium" seats, most of which, the Yankees say, will sell for "less than $100."

If the Yankees' fondest wish comes true, the vast majority of seats in the new stadium will be purchased by season-ticket holders. But no matter what happens, the shared experience of parents taking their children to a baseball game will become less common. Only the rich will be able to do it on a regular basis. Some parents won't be able to do it at all.

The new Yankee message isn't "bring your kids." It's "bring your clients."

Shea Stadium will also be demolished at the end of the year. But that's not much of a loss. 1964 (when Shea opened) isn't 1923. And there was never any grandeur to Shea. Not even Mets fans have an emotional attachment to it.

Yankee Stadium is different. The Yankees earned thirty-seven American League pennants and twenty-six World Series championships while playing there. But let's face reality. Over the centuries, there has been a standard operating procedure for invaders, whether from Mongolia (like Genghis Khan) or Cleveland (George Steinbrenner). First, they occupy and pillage a temple. Then they destroy it.

Baseball is a game of tradition. It lives in large measure on its past. No matter how one styles the facts, the destruction of the original Yankee Stadium will bury another piece of baseball history. The Bronx Bombers might make more money over the next thirty years than they would have if they'd stayed put. But there will be one less link to that glorious era when baseball was truly America's national pastime.

Indeed, the Yankees might find themselves haunted by angry ghosts as a consequence of demolishing "The House that Ruth Built." For more than four decades, "The Curse of The Bambino" afflicted the Boston Red Sox. Maybe the coming years will witness a new curse. Ghosts don't relocate on command.

Meanwhile, on the evening of May 6, I said good-bye to a old friend.

The Yankees were playing the Cleveland Indians. It was a perfect night for baseball; warm with a gentle breeze.

The sky was clear when the game began and turned cobalt blue as the night wore on.

The players looked very young to me.

Andy Pettitte pitched into the seventh inning for the Yankees and left the game with a 3–2 lead. Joba Chamberlain came on in relief, walked two men, and surrendered a three-run homer to David Dellucci. The Indians won 5-to-3.

When the game was over, I walked to the concourse beneath the stands. Then, on impulse, I turned around and retraced my steps for one last look at the emerald-green field and massive stands that meant so much to me when I was young.

I was still moved by the majesty of it all.

As William Wordsworth wrote many years ago, "The child is father of the man."

Long Ago at Madison Square Garden

On October 26, 1961, I went to a Knicks game at Madison Square Garden. I know the date because I still have the program. It was part of an NBA doubleheader. That should give you an idea of how the National Basketball Association has changed.

In autumn 1961, the NBA consisted of nine teams. Its brightest stars were Wilt Chamberlain, Bill Russell, Oscar Robertson, Elgin Baylor, and Jerry West. Chamberlain would defy belief that year by playing all but eight minutes of the entire season for the Philadelphia Warriors and averaging 50.4 points per game. Robertson averaged a triple-double with 30.8 points, 12.5 rebounds, and 11.4 assists. Russell led the Boston Celtics to the fourth of what would ultimately be eight consecutive NBA crowns.

Madison Square Garden was located at the time on Eighth Avenue between 49th and 50th Streets. The Knicks had thirty-three home games, seventeen of which were part of doubleheaders. Ticket prices ranged from $5.00 down to $1.50. I was fifteen years old; the same age as the NBA.

I don't recall much about the first game of the doubleheader on October 26, except that it was between the Syracuse Nationals and St. Louis Hawks. But I remember very clearly a moment that occurred midway through the third quarter. Wayne Embry, who would be playing center for the Cincinnati Royals in the nightcap, walked into the arena and stood just inside the entrance curtain. He was in uniform, watching the action.

Nothing ventured; nothing gained. I left my seat in the balcony and went downstairs with my program. The corridors weren't hard to navigate. Minutes later, pen in hand, I was standing next to Embry and a teammate who had joined him.

"Excuse me; Mr. Embry. Could I have your autograph?"

Embry signed my program and I handed it to the second player.

"Could I have your autograph too, please?"

"If you know who I am."

That was a problem, since I had no idea who he was. Then a miraculous vision appeared. Oscar Robertson walked through the curtain and stopped beside us to watch the ongoing game.

"He wants your autograph," Mr. Anonymous told Robertson.

"What's your name?" Robertson queried.

"Tom."

"Robertson took my pen and program and wrote, "To Tom, O Robertson."

"Do you still want mine?" the anonymous player asked.

"Yes."

That's how I got Bob Boozer's autograph. And every other member of the Cincinnati Royals team.

Knowing a good thing, I held my ground when the Knicks and Royals took the court and waited for the players from the first game. All told, I got twenty-seven signatures, including future Hall of Famers Bob Pettit, Clyde Lovellette, Jack Twyman, Dolph Schayes, and Hal Greer.

Two months later, on Christmas night, I returned to the Garden. This time, the first match-up was between the Detroit Pistons and Chicago Packers, with the Knicks taking on the Philadelphia Warriors in the second game.

The Knicks were heavy underdogs. They would finish in last place that season. Philadelphia was led by Wilt Chamberlain, who would score an incredible one hundred points against them in a single game two months later. But it was Christmas, and the Knicks won in double overtime. I still remember 6 foot, 5 inch Johnny Green, who was forced to guard Chamberlain after both Knicks centers fouled out, cradling the ball in his arms at the final buzzer. I got twenty-nine more autographs that evening, including future Hall of Famers Walter Bellamy and Paul Arizin.

Four nights later, the Boston Celtics were in town and I was at the Garden again. By now, I'd learned to arrive early and position myself between the locker rooms to stop players as they came in. I'd also brought some color pictures torn from *Sport* magazine.

Red Auerbach's signature was my first acquisition. Frank Ramsey and K. C. Jones followed. Then I saw Bill Russell walking toward me. There was an aura about him. The image of an eagle flashed through my mind. He was carrying a large gym bag.

"Mr. Russell. Could you sign this picture for me?"

Russell kept walking.

"Please; I'll hold your bag."

Wordlessly, Russell shifted the bag to his other hand, took my picture in the same hand, reached for my pen, and signed. I later learned that he didn't give out autographs. To this day, I don't know why he signed.

That gave me seventy signatures on three programs along with several signed photos.

Four months later, on the afternoon of May 19, 1962, my grandmother called. That night, there would be a gala fundraiser at Madison Square Garden to celebrate John F. Kennedy's birthday. The president would be there. The list of performers included Ella Fitzgerald, Jimmy Durante, Maria Callas, Jack Benny, Peggy Lee, Danny Kaye, and Bobby Darin. A client had given my grandfather four tickets. Would I like to come with a friend?

We arrived early, and I decided to put my basketball experience to the test. Soon, I was standing outside one of the visiting-team locker rooms. The door was wide open. Ella Fitzgerald was alone inside. I still have my "Birthday Salute to President Kennedy" program with her signature on it.

Then the president arrived, security tightened, and it was suggested that I return to my seat, which I did for the start of the show. That was the night Marilyn Monroe put on her sequined gown and sang "Happy Birthday" to the president of the United States.

My autograph collecting continued through high school. Then I went off to college and got "too old" to stand outside locker rooms. But during my freshman year of college, I returned to the Garden, pen in hand, one last time.

It was November 26, 1963; four days after the assassination of President Kennedy. I was devastated. Kennedy had been my childhood hero.

The mood at the Garden was somber that night. I did my thing. The signatures I collected went into a closet with previously gathered autographs and other keepsakes that I would hold onto and, in truth, not look at very often over the years.

Thereafter, times changed. They always do. Kids can no longer stand outside locker rooms and get autographs from NBA stars. Meanwhile, I continued through life, became an attorney and author, and made new friends. One of those friends is Tom Hoover.

The record book shows that Tom Hoover played parts of three seasons in the NBA. He was in one hundred games, scored 350 points, and
logged eleven minutes of playoff time. He was listed as 6 feet, 10 inches
tall (a height he still claims), but I think he's closer to 6-8. He's also a
good person. It's an honor to be his friend.

Recently, I decided to look at my old Knick programs. Some of the
signatures are hard to decipher, but most are easy to read. There's Bob
Wiesenhahn, Barney Cable, John Rudometkin, and Swede Halbrook. Also
Johnny Kerr, Al Attles, Richie Guerin, and Don Nelson. On the cover of
the program dated November 26, 1963, in handwriting more legible than
most, is the legend "Tom Hoover."

I don't remember his signing. But I know that, when he signed, it was
important to me.